Tarrant on Millionaires

The Mad, Bad World of the Filthy Rich

Tarrant
on Millionaires

The Mad, Bad World of the Filthy Rich

CHRIS TARRANT
with Mark Leigh and Mike Lepine

Illustrations by Larry

HarperCollins*Entertainment*
An Imprint of HarperCollins*Publishers*

HarperCollins*Entertainment*
An Imprint of HarperCollins*Publishers*
77–85 Fulham Palace Road,
Hammersmith, London W6 8JB

www.**fire**and**water**.com

This paperback edition 1999

1 3 5 7 9 8 6 4 2

First published in Great Britain by
HarperCollins*Entertainment* 1999

ISBN 0 00 653193 8

Set in Tekton and Perpetua

Printed and bound in Great Britain by
Clays Ltd, St Ives plc

Contents

Acknowledgments

The authors would like to thank the following people for their invaluable help and assistance: Jenny Allsop, Mary Hatton, Philippa Hatton-Lepine, Gage Hatton-Lepine, Andrea Henry, Colin Higgs, Val Hudson, Barney Leigh, Debbie Leigh, Polly Leigh, Judy Martin and Julie Smith.

Introduction

Amazing stuff, money ... The very large majority of people find it almost impossible to acquire in the first place. A few gain it by having the right idea at exactly the right time, and having the courage to act on it. For some, their vast quantities of money are due to sheer hard work and investment, and yet for others, the wealth they have just gets greater and greater without their really trying! Once they've got it, its increase is just a natural and inevitable process. For example, if you were worth the colossal sum of £1 million in 1900, you would now be worth nearly £53 million. The richest man in England in 1900 was Cecil Rhodes, the diamond merchant, who was then reckoned to be worth £50 million. Today that figure would have escalated to £3.5 billion.

A hundred years earlier, the eighth richest man in Britain was Richard Arkwright, whose dad invented the spinning jenny. His cotton fortune was believed to be worth about £1 million. Today's value of his fortune would be more like £120 million. The rise in value is very fast. The Duke of Westminster was worth an enormous £40 million in 1950. Today that would equate to £800 million. 1950 was also the year in which my granddad – not a particularly rich man but one who had a hatred of banks and building societies that I've inherited from him – bought his house outright for the mind-numbing sum of £1,000!

These days, there are more millionaires, multimillionaires and billionaires than ever before and only 30% of them now get their money from inherited wealth – a figure that is going down all the time. The top 1,000 richest men and women in England in 1999 had a total estimated wealth between them of £115 billion. This is a mind-boggling amount of money; all the more so when you appreciate that less than 1% of the population of Great Britain earns over £100,000 a year.

The super rich get their money in all sorts of different ways. Hans Rausing – the food packaging tycoon – is currently the richest man in Britain, worth an estimated £3,400 million. And that's gone up in just one year from £2,800 million in 1998 – not a bad twelve months for him, was it ?

By contrast, the second richest man in the UK, Lord Sainsbury, saw his fortune drop in value in 1999. The poor love has had to muddle by on just £3,100 million – down from £3,300 million – in the last twelve months. What sort of a life can it be for someone when you lose £200 million in a year? When you're talking these kinds of figures, probably still a pretty good one!

Paul McCartney is one of the many people who have made a huge amount of money from recording and writing music. Paul's fortune is estimated at £500 million. Andrew Lloyd Webber is worth about £350 million; Sir Elton John is worth an estimated £160 million; Mick Jagger, almost a pauper by comparison, is only worth £150 million (but don't tell Jerry!); and David Bowie is positively skint with just £100 million to get by on the best he can. It seems that any sort of musical entertainment can bring in big bucks to a talented few. Michael Flatley has amassed £50 million just from being Lord of the Dance.

There's money to be made in the movies as well. Even twenty years ago, Marlon Brando got £3 million for a paltry two days' work on *Superman*. Jack Nicholson got £3 million for just ten days work on *A Few Good Men* (this worked out at £400 a minute for his actual time), and Jolly Jack also got £28 million for his role as the Joker in *Batman*, thanks to a profit-sharing deal. Sean Connery got $1 million for one day's work on *Robin Hood, Prince of Thieves*, and Bruce Willis got £1.7 million for a week's work on *Billy Bathgate*. (If you've seen the film it'll be clear that the producers should have saved their money!) Whitney Houston recorded a TV ad for a Japanese financial firm at the rate of £200,000 per word! She raked in £1 million for uttering, 'Make it happen with Nissan.' Sport is another area where sponsorship, prize money are just going up and up, as are the profits. Bernie Ecclestone has made £900 million from motor racing, and Martin Edwards, the chairman of Manchester United FC, is worth £115 million. The highest paid British sportsmen in the last twelve months were Damon Hill (£6.9 million), Lennox Lewis (£5.4 million) and Prince Naseem (£4.5 million). Tennis players, footballers and golfers will feature more and more in the rich lists over the next decade.

Combining the worlds of pop music and sport, David Beckham and his wife, Posh Spice, formerly known as Victoria Adams, already have a fortune of over £20 million. Baby Brooklyn will be the heir to a very large fortune when Mum and Dad finally decide to take life in the slow lane.

More and more people are also making money from the hi-tech world that we live in – an increasing number of millionaires are earning their money from computers, the internet and the mobile phone. Charles Dunstan, the boss of Carphone Warehouse, is worth an estimated £130 million, and Alan Sugar has made £260 million from a mixture of electronics and football.

For a long time the richest woman in Britain, Her Majesty the Queen now has to suffer the indignity of knowing that eighty-six of her subjects are worth more money than she is. She has to get by as best she can on a paltry £250 million.

Paul Raymond has earned more than double that from encouraging girls to get their kit off in public places; Marco Pierre

White has amassed £50 million from cooking and running high-class restaurants; and Anne Wood is reckoned to be worth over £55 million, all thanks to having created children's programmes 'Rosie and Jim' and 'The Teletubbies'!

People continue to make money in the most unlikely ways. Turkey maestro Bernard Matthews, now worth in excess of £70 million, was once an insurance salesman who, in 1953, splashed out £2.50 on twenty turkey eggs and a paraffin oil incubator – a little venture that turned out rather well for him. Percy Shaw became a multimillionaire from that driving aid the cats-eye. Ron Hickman earned millions from the Black & Decker Workmate. And Ako Morita got so fed up having to listen to pop music blaring out from his children's record player that he sat down and invented the Sony Walkman. It has made him many millions!

Life turned out pretty good for George Soros too. A former waiter and dishwasher, he made something believed to be not far short of a £1,000 million on the stock market in just one day in 1992: Black Wednesday.

Of course, some people aren't very good at keeping hold of their money. Kevin Maxwell, one of the sons of disgraced tycoon Robert, became Britain's biggest bankrupt with debts of £406 million, and banker Nick Leeson lost Barings Bank £850 million in illegal trading before he was discovered and imprisoned in February 1995. He had swerved off £25 million into his own bank account in the first six months of 1994.

A lot of other people lose their cash in the divorce courts. Neil Diamond paid his ex-wife Marcia £100 million by way of settlement but, amazingly, and very untypically of the moneyed, said he was perfectly happy to do so because she had contributed greatly to the success of his career. James Cameron, director of *Titanic*, is being taken for it as fast as it's coming in to the tune of £80 million by his ex-wife Linda Hamilton. Steven Spielberg paid Amy Irving £72.4 million; Roseanne Barr paid Tom Arnold £33 million; Kevin

Costner paid Cindy Costner £25 million; Phil Collins paid Jill Collins £25 million; and billionaire property developer Donald Trump got off rather lightly, giving Ivana only £16 million.

And it's not only in the divorce courts that money flows freely – a lot of people have lost a lot of money to lawyers. Actor Bill Roache, aka Ken Barlow in 'Coronation Street', who actually won his case against the *Sun* newspaper for their libellous comment that he was the most boring man on TV, has now had to declare himself bankrupt as he couldn't afford to pay the huge costs of the case. Completely the opposite thing happened to Barbara Carlisle and her family. Living in rural Alabama, they discovered that they had been overcharged £750 by a door to door salesman for their satellite TV dish. They were understandably outraged and, in the best American tradition, sued. But even they were amazed at the damages awarded by the jury … an incomprehensible £363 million!

The US legal system is clearly out of control. Consider too that this is the same country where a tribunal awarded £2.5 million to a doctor who did not like the paint used to touch up his new BMW.

The housing market too has gone berserk. Over 200 people in Britain have bought houses worth over £2 million in the past twelve months. And the new record for the most expensive house ever purchased in Britain was set this year when a ten-bedroomed house in Kensington was put on the market for £35 million. The stamp duty alone would be £1,225,000 … But at those prices, who's counting the odd million or so?

Of course, being a millionaire isn't all that it's cracked up to be if you live in a different part of the world. In the States, a dollar millionaire is only worth about £600,000 sterling. In France, a franc millionaire and in South Africa, a rand millionaire are both only worth about £100,000. In Malta, on the other hand, a million lire is actually worth £1.6 million UK pounds – but that's rather exceptional. In most countries, millionaires are worth considerably less than in the UK. In India a rupee millionaire is only worth about

£14,000. In Italy a lire millionaire – and presumably that's everybody in the country – is worth about £350, and in Turkey a lire millionaire is worth the princely sum of £1.63.

The richest man in the world continues to be Bill Gates, the boss of Microsoft, who could live very well indeed in Turkey and manages to live pretty well in the USA too. At current estimates he's worth around $71 billion … This means he's worth more than the Gross Domestic Product of Egypt, Pakistan and Ireland. He could buy 460 Boeing 747s, 208,000 brand new Bentley Continentals and 7.1 billion Viagra tablets. If Bill takes one per day, they'll last him 53,863 years. He should become a trillionaire by December 2004 and be able to pay off the entire US National Debt on 21 July 2008. His wealth brings him an estimated daily income of £30 million – that's £20,833 a minute … But is he happy?!

Chris Tarrant

Chapter 1

CAN'T BUY ME LOVE

' *If women didn't exist, all the money in the world would have no meaning.*
— Aristotle Onassis '

The more lives of the rich and famous one uncovers, the more clear it is that a lot of money really doesn't make a lot of people very happy. In fact, often, quite the reverse is true. Despite their millions, people still can't find love, so they can't even kid themselves any longer that if only they were rich they'd be a lot more attractive and have a lot more friends.

For example, when she inherited her father's fortune in 1975, Christina Onassis received a yearly income estimated at $50 million. Some of this money was used to buy friends – she didn't have many of her own, so she paid people by the week to be houseguests. She had a craving for Diet Coke and reportedly drank up to twenty-four bottles a day. When she found herself in a country where her favourite drink was not available, she would send her private jet to buy a supply.

After she had divorced her fourth husband, Thierry Roussel, the father of her daughter, she begged him for a sample of his sperm in order that she could have another child. At first he said no, but then changed his mind when he heard what she had to offer in exchange – a new Ferrari Testarossa.

£ Notorious skinflint W. C. Fields was absolutely paranoid that his wife, Carlotta, was stealing from him and would leave piles of money around the house to test her. From time to time Carlotta would add a $5 bill to one of the piles, just to confuse him.

Fields also hired a detective to follow her to make sure she wasn't seeing anyone else. Carlotta, realising she was being followed, drove around aimlessly for hours on end, knowing that her husband was being charged by the mile.

Her plan worked. As soon as Fields saw his first bill, he fired the detective.

£ Aimee Semple McPherson was, in her day, one of America's best loved Evangelists. She made millions from her shows, which owed as much to Hollywood as to the Bible, and treated herself to fabulous jewellery and couturier clothes from the donations given by the faithful. She based her operations in Los Angeles, building the 'Angelus Temple' there in 1923 at a cost of £1.5 million. Its single most tasteful feature was a giant illuminated revolving red cross, which could be seen up to fifty miles away. There was also a radio station, a museum of miracles containing the discarded crutches and wheelchairs of all those she had healed and a 5,000-seat auditorium. Aimee's sure-fire formula mixed positive religious messages with show-business and American patriotism. She didn't preach parables – she acted them out with a troupe of actors and spectacular scenery, and the show would close to the waving of the Stars and Stripes. Little did her many devout followers know that she had an apartment she called the 'Frat Flat' where she would 'fraternise with the faithful' – as long as they were young, good looking and male … She described her ideal man as 'a trombone player'. Lord only knows what on earth she meant by that …

Aimee was at the height of her popularity – and then things started to crash down about her ears. In 1926, she disappeared while sunbathing on a beach in Los Angeles. Immediately the word went out that she had been swept out to sea and a massive search party was organised. Two swimmers died in the search and a third person committed suicide from grief. But Aimee hadn't drowned. A month later a note turned up at her temple. She had been kidnapped and would be freed for a sum of $500,000. Before anyone could act, Aimee turned up again, this time in Mexico, claiming she'd been held prisoner by a group calling themselves 'The Avengers'. God, she said, had helped her to escape. The police were sceptical. They couldn't find any trace of the kidnappers or their hideout, and Aimee didn't look the least bit upset by her ordeal. Then witnesses started to come forward, saying they'd seen her hanging out in a hotel with a married man. The police were determined to bring charges against her, suspecting a big sting, and it took all the influence of her good friend, newspaper tycoon Randolph Hearst, to get them to change their minds and free her.

Aimee's career never really recovered from the scandal, and she finally took an overdose of sleeping pills in 1944. She was buried with a telephone in her coffin so that she could report back from Heaven. After seven years without a single tinkle, the phone line was finally disconnected ...

> '**When you don't have any money, the problem is food.**
> **When you have money, it's sex.**
> **When you have both, it's health.'**
> **– J. P. Donleavy**

£ Blackpool's Merseyside estate was definitely the place to be in August 1998. A mystery woman stuffed £440 into the hands of a ten-year-old boy before proceeding to post thousands more pounds through people's letterboxes and windows. When challenged, the woman said she'd recently won £3.1 million on a lottery but was giving it all away because nobody loved her ...

> '**A sex symbol becomes a thing. I hate being a thing.'**
> **– Marilyn Monroe**

£ 'Pig Faced Dugan' was a millionaire in the 1930s who was convinced that, despite his bloated, porcine appearance, his money would make him attractive to women. He was wrong. After numerous rebuttals from women you'd have thought he would have got used to it but he still took offence every single time. When one particular woman rejected him, he decided to get his revenge by ruining all those closest to her. Using his immense wealth, he first set about destroying her father's business. Next he turned his attention to her boyfriend and his father, ruining them and causing the father to commit suicide. All through his campaign Dugan kept pestering the girl – but still she refused to have anything to do with him.

Eventually the girl and her boyfriend decided to get their own back. Contacting everyone who held a grudge against

Dugan (and there were hundreds) the couple arranged for them to send him thousands of pictures of pigs. They began to arrive at his house on a daily basis – letters and packages containing drawings, prints, engravings and photographs of pigs. There was even a huge oil painting of a pig whose face had been replaced by that of Dugan.

This all became too much for the millionaire. In 1938, in his office, surrounded by all the pig pictures, he shot himself.

. A sinister gemstone seems to have been responsible for the deaths of more rich people than champagne, syphilis and hunting accidents combined.

The Hope Diamond, which is said to hypnotise its wealthy owners with its strange deep blue light, left its first owner, Sir Francis Hope, destitute. To pay his many debts, he sold it to a French financier – who later went mad and killed himself. Many subsequent owners died sudden and brutal deaths. The diamond was owned, most notoriously, by King Louis XVI and Marie

Antoinette, both of whom died on the guillotine. Marie Antoinette's close friend, the Princesse de Lamballe, who had once borrowed the diamond, was literally torn to pieces by a Parisian street mob.

In 1908, the diamond surfaced once again and was sold to the Russian Prince Kanitouski as a gift for his mistress, Mademoiselle Ladue, a star of the Folies Bergères. She was shot to death shortly afterwards by a spurned lover, and the Prince himself died two days later, stabbed to death by a madman while out walking in the streets of Paris.

The next the world saw of the Hope Diamond, it had come into the possession of Sultan Abdul Hamid of Turkey. He gave it to his favourite wife – and then shot her dead. Soon after, he was deposed in a political coup. The jewel passed on to a Greek broker, who was killed with his wife and child when their horse and carriage inexplicably bolted into a deep precipice.

In 1911, Washington society hostess Evelyn Walsh McClean saw the stone in Cartier's and begged her husband, *Washington Post* newspaper tycoon Edward McClean, to buy it for her. She said she was mesmerised by the blue light inside. Before her life was over, she would have ample cause to believe in the curse of the Hope Diamond. Her son died in a motor accident, her husband ended up in a mental asylum and two of her friends who had borrowed the gem died strange and unaccountable deaths. When she herself died, addicted to drink and drugs, she willed the gemstone to her six grandchildren – on the condition that they never touched it. Eventually, the cursed jewel was given to the Smithsonian Institute, where it remains safely to this day …

£ Florida socialite Louise Stanton inherited her husband's fortune when he died in a car crash in 1933. But although she had everything, his widow couldn't

face life without him. Just two weeks after his death she borrowed an aircraft, filled it with four hours' worth of fuel and set off due east over the Atlantic. At around this time a friend found a note that she had left. It read, 'I'm just going into space to find out what it's all about. If there isn't anything that will be OK too.'

Neither the plane nor Mrs Stanton were ever found.

. William Randolph Hearst's mother once said that as a boy, every time her son felt bad, he would go out and buy himself something to cheer him up.

If that's true, then the adult Hearst must have been the most miserable man on earth, because he spent money like it was going out of fashion. Almost on a whim, he purchased and imported an entire Spanish monastery and Bavarian village over to America to be rebuilt there, and collected over 20,000 art treasures in his lifetime. At one time, it was estimated that Hearst was buying one in every four art treasures on sale in the world. He hoarded them away, and often forgot to unpack them from their crates. Certainly, the Spanish monastery was left in its boxes for almost fifteen years without being opened.

Expensive as these purchases were, they positively pale into insignificance compared to the money he laid out on his dream home, San Simeon, a 130-room, eighty-seven-bathroom castle built on 240,000 acres over twenty-five years at a cost of around $30 million. To give you a proper idea of the size, the estate, located on the coast between Los Angeles and San Francisco, is larger than Bedfordshire. Hearst called it 'My little hideaway on my little hilltop.'

Everything – and I mean everything – about San Simeon was over the top. It was furnished with an array of treasures which included King Charles I's bed and personal effects.

An inventory of the antiques listed 6,776 items and included priceless Greek statues and vases, over 5,000 books, and paintings by Van Dyck and Rembrandt.

Those lucky enough to enjoy Hearst's hospitality travelled there on a private train and were then transported the final six miles on a private highway that crossed San Simeon. Although his personal and business ethics were as low as a snake's belly, Hearst was a great animal lover. San Simeon also featured a zoo and wild animals were left to wander freely through the grounds (mouse traps were banned from the grounds and every room).

P. G. Wodehouse was a guest once and wrote about the zoo, 'The specimens considered reasonably harmless are allowed to roam at large. You are apt to meet a bear or two before you get to the house, or an elephant, or even Sam Goldwyn.'

In fact anyone who was anyone was summoned to stay at San Simeon with Hearst. Few turned down the invitation because of its prestige. They recognised that spending time with Hearst himself would be the price they would have to pay for the privilege. Hearst was feared by many and loved by few. 'The man has not a friend in the world,' said the writer Ambrose Bierce. 'Nor does he deserve one.'

The man who had bought himself one of the largest homes in the world died alone in 1951, aged eighty-eight.

'The rich who are unhappy are worse off than the poor who are unhappy; for the poor at least cling to the hope that more money would solve their problems, but the rich know better.' – Sidney Harris

When the Monty Python team visited America they were stunned to get an invitation from Elvis to come and visit him at Graceland. They were even more surprised when 'the King' started performing their sketches in front of them! By all accounts Elvis did a particularly excellent Gumby impression! His own life, of course, was even stranger than any Monty Python sketch, combining acts of gross generosity, gross indecency and gross ill temperament.

Here was a man who liked to visit the Memphis City morgue to look at the corpses, who enjoyed watching couples having sex through special two-way mirrors and who believed he was in telepathic contact with his dead twin Jesse who had died at birth.

He also believed he was being haunted by the ghost of his mother Gladys, would happily fly 1,000 miles for his favourite peanut butter sandwich and enjoyed discharging loaded firearms into walls, furniture and television sets. It would have made a great Monty Python sketch if it hadn't been so tragic.

Elvis grossed more than a billion dollars in his lifetime. Colonel Tom Parker hadn't been kidding when he said in 1956, 'You stay talented and sexy and I'll make us amazing deals that will make us both as rich as rajahs ...'

Incidentally, Elvis earned himself his first million before he was twenty-one, so Parker was right!

> **Whenever Joan Crawford remarried, she changed the name of her home and replaced all the toilet seats.**

. In Paris in the mid-1800s, a little redheaded English girl named Cora Pearl made herself a millionairess by going out with the wealthiest men she could find. She called them her 'golden chain of lovers'. Her charms must have been considerable because they paid for her three magnificent houses, a stable of sixty horses and showered her with jewels worth over one million francs. She was quite blatant about only seeing them for their money and jotted down everything each one gave her to see who was worth keeping sweet.

Once a millionaire hotelier named Alexander Duvall fell deeply in love with Cora and wrote to her, 'Will you let me prove my devotion? Command me and I will die!' Cora swiftly wrote back saying, 'I would rather you live and pay my bills!' Another besotted lover, James Whelpley, gave her his entire fortune. She spent the lot in just two months – and then gave him the boot. She got through two million francs of Prince Napoleon's personal fortune and another admirer sent her a huge silver horse, filled to the brim inside with jewels and gold coins.

Then things started to go wrong. The hotelier who had volunteered to die for her turned up on her doorstep – and promptly shot himself. The scandal ruined her in Paris and people started to avoid her. A lifelong gambling addict, she threw away what she had amassed on the gaming tables of Europe and died poor and alone in a cheap and dirty boarding house.

She was all set for a pauper's funeral when a mystery man turned up and paid for her to be buried in the style in which she had lived her life. Some gentleman was paying her bills for her, right to the very last ...

> 'Nobody works as hard for his money as the man who marries for it.'– Kin Hubbard

Mrs Ronald Greville, heiress to a Scottish brewing fortune, was extremely jealous of any guests whose jewellery was grander than hers. After a dinner party one of her guests, a rich American lady, discovered that a large diamond had fallen out of her necklace. The other guests got down on the carpet to help search for the missing stone – all except Mrs Greville. She left the room, only to reappear a few minutes later holding a magnifying glass and announcing, 'Perhaps this will help.'

£ Long before Viagra there was Doctor John 'Goat Gland' Brinkley to turn to if you weren't quite feeling up to your marital obligations. Dr John – he bought the doctorate by mail order – was an audacious American con man who claimed he could cure impotence by surgically implanting goats' testicles into his patients for $750 a time. For $1,500 he'd insert an entire young goat's member. 'Just let me get your goat and you'll be a Ram-What-Am with every lamb!' his advertisements promised. Potency was 'Guaranteed by God's most virile creatures!'

Dr John got the idea while working at a slaughterhouse. He saw how many sets of goats' tackle there were knocking around and thought he could find a better use for them than putting them in sausages.

Some of the most affluent men of the time flocked (excuse the pun) to Dr John's surgery to have goats' testes implanted in them, and the Maharaja Thakou of Morvi raced all the way from India to get his treatment. The American Medical Association branded Dr John 'a giant in quackery', but that didn't stop him becoming a multi-millionaire. By the 1920s, he had his own radio station, numerous Cadillacs, a yacht and a private plane. When criticism from the American Medical Association got too hot, Dr John decamped to Mexico and peddled his treatments there until he died of a heart attack aged fifty-six.

And no, the treatment didn't work.

> **'No rich man is ugly.'**
> **– Zsa Zsa Gabor**

. Virtually the first words Woolworth heiress Barbara Hutton heard from her first husband on their honeymoon were, 'Barbara, you're too damn fat ... now let's get down to business!' Hardly surprising, then, that her marriage to Prince Alexis Mdivani didn't last long. He was hardly perfect either, and had the rather unattractive habit of lying on his back, screaming and kicking his arms and legs in the air when he didn't get his own way.

Despite this, Barbara took his cruel words to heart and embarked upon a course of chain smoking and violent eating disorders which were to wreck her life and all her marriages. She married two more princes, a baron and another husband made her a countess. She had seven marriages in all, one to notorious skinflint Cary Grant – whom she managed to traumatise by her spending sprees – and one to a very obviously homosexual German tennis player who kept going away on extended 'business trips'. None of her seven marriages lasted very long ...

American railroad baron Jim Brady tried to woo actress Lillian Russell with a most unusual gift – a gold-plated bicycle encrusted with precious jewels. It failed.

When Aristotle Onassis came to marry Jacqueline Kennedy in 1968, a marriage agreement was drawn up consisting of no less than 173 separate clauses! It agreed that the couple could have separate bedrooms, that they only had to spend Catholic and summer holidays together and that no children were to be born. The future Mrs Onassis was guaranteed an income of £21,000 a month, of which £6,000 was to be in clothes. If she changed her mind and wanted a divorce in the first five years of marriage, Jacqueline would receive a sum of £12 million – and if he left her she'd receive £6 million for every year they'd been together.

Alexander Onassis said of his father's wedding to Jackie Kennedy: 'It's a perfect match. My father loves names and Jackie loves money.'

Sarah Winchester inherited the $20 million fortune made by her father-in-law William, inventor of the Winchester repeating rifle – the gun that won the West. She was one of the wealthiest women in America but money couldn't buy her happiness. After her husband and her child died, Sarah visited a medium in Boston who warned her that they had been murdered by the ghosts of all those who had been killed by Winchester rifles. These thousands of angry spirits, said the medium, would eventually kill Sarah too.

The only way to avoid this curse, Sarah was told, was to build a vast labyrinth of a home that would confuse the spirits and keep her safe from them. If they ever found their way through the house, the medium said, they would devour Sarah. Whatever happened, Sarah would have to keep building the house and making its layout more and more complicated and illogical. Because, if she ever stopped, her time would come …

Strange advice – but Sarah was so scared by the curse that she believed it. She started building a mansion on six acres near San Jose in California. A whole team of builders and craftsmen worked non-stop, twenty-four hours a day, seven days a week. Sarah designed the house herself, fearful that any stoppage would allow the ghosts into her home. She built for the sake of it.

Doors opened on to blank brick walls. Rooms were built within rooms. Staircases and corridors led nowhere. Sarah deliberately built booby traps too, with doors that suddenly opened on to deep air shafts.

By the time she'd finished, the Winchester Mansion had more than 160 rooms, 2,000 doors, 10,000 windows – and forty-seven chimneys, we think. No one knows for sure. Sarah was also obsessed with the number thirteen, so the house had thirteen bathrooms, thirteen hooks in every cupboard and thirteen candles in every chandelier. The sewing room had thirteen windows and thirteen doors.

The construction – and the torment – finally stopped when Sarah died in 1922 aged eighty-two, thirty-eight years and $5 million after the work began. Even her will had thirteen parts to it and she dutifully signed it thirteen times.

It was actress Joan Peters who first noticed that her billionaire husband Howard Hughes was going a little strange. After their wedding, he insisted that they had separate beds – and separate fridges. She was never allowed to cook for him. Each night, he prepared himself exactly the same meal of steak, salad and peas, and then spent a considerable time checking on the size of each pea. Any pea that was considered too big would be flicked away in disgust.

The marriage soon deteriorated along with Hughes's mental state. The papers started to get wind of what was happening and Hughes tried to explain. He told a journalist, 'Everybody carries germs around with them. I want to live longer than my parents, so I avoid germs ...' His morbid fear of germs was something he had inherited from his mother.

Hughes became a hermit in 1958, aged fifty–three, going into virtual seclusion in the ninth–floor penthouse of the Desert Inn Hotel in Las Vegas. To ensure his privacy he had the lift buttons altered so that they only indicated eight floors. Suffering from a phobia and paranoia about germs Hughes soon would not touch anything unless he was protected by a paper tissue. He even walked around with his feet in empty tissue boxes to stop them from coming into contact with the floor. The windows were painted black because he was worried about being affected by sunlight. To ensure he had no physical contact with his staff, they were separated by a glass wall and spoken to via an intercom.

Sadly, as he aged, his mind deteriorated further. He started to collect all his urine and keep it in large jars. His every moment was watched over by his 'Mormon Mafia' bodyguards. Everything had to be sterilised before he would touch it and he employed men to catch flies in his rooms. According to those few who actually met him, he 'stank like a skunk' and wore the same clothes for months on end – or just his underpants. His claw-like nails grew to two inches in length and his hair hung down to his chest and was rarely combed. When it was, he insisted on using a new comb after every three strokes … Even his doctors were only ever allowed to examine him from the far side of the room.

Before he died, Hughes spent years in seclusion in a succession of darkened hotel rooms, being carried on a stretcher from hotel to hotel, from continent to continent. Wherever he went his drivers were instructed to drive square in the middle of the road regardless of the consequences, to stay as far as possible away from the gutters. Once in his new hotel, he would sit naked, except for a paper napkin, singing his favourite old–time jazz songs, or watching his favourite movie, *Ice Station Zebra*, over and over and over and over again – with the sound turned up so loud the walls literally shook. It was the sad end to a dashing and brilliant career.

At the end, the man who had once been 6' 4" in his prime

was so emaciated and sick that he weighed just 90lbs and was described as looking like 'a frail, long-legged child'. What finally killed the richest man in the United States in March 1976, aged seventy, as he was being transported in one of his private jets, was a combination of kidney failure and tertiary syphilis.

£ Although for tens of thousands of people money is the key to a genuinely better life, free at last from debt and daily worries, it is amazing how many people become thoroughly miserable on winning or inheriting large sums of money.

Buddy Post, for example, won $16.2 million on the Pennsylvania State Lottery in 1988. Since then his wife Constance has left him, he's served two years in jail for assaulting his step-daughter's boyfriend in an argument over business, his brother Jeffrey has been convicted of trying to murder him for the money, his business went bust and the gas company cut off supplies to his mansion after he was declared bankrupt with debts of $500,000 ....

Chapter 2

GENEROUS TO A FAULT

Viewing the matter in retrospect, I can testify that it is nearly always easier to make one million dollars honestly than to dispose of it wisely.
— *Julius Rosenwald*

For some people, earning money seems to be almost too easy. But the ability to use it sensibly, usefully or wisely is completely beyond them. For example, Woo Tai Ling, a Chinese millionaire from Shanghai, had a nightmare in which he couldn't squeeze through the narrow gates of Heaven because of all his money bags. The very next day, he gave away every last penny of his fortune and went to work as a market porter.

💰 The Sultan of Brunei must be one of the biggest tippers in the world. After a short stay at the Four Seasons Hotel in Cyprus in 1973 he left the staff a $170,000 tip with a note reading, 'This is a small token of my appreciation.'

Similarly, the Saudi Arabian Oil Minister Sheikh al-Yamani once tipped a barber $300 for giving him a good shave.

💷 **Millionaire James Gordon Bennett's tipping was legendary. He once gave a guard on a train from Paris a tip of $14,000. The man waited until the train reached its destination and then immediately resigned.**

Bennett was always trying to get rid of money. He was seen on one occasion throwing thousand-franc notes into a fire just because he couldn't get seated comfortably in an armchair with such a wad in his pockets.

💰. Victor Emmanuel II was famous for two things. The first was being the first king to rule over a united Italy. The second was for giving gifts that were extremely valuable but also extremely vulgar.

The gifts in question were clippings of his big toe nail, which he let go untrimmed for a whole year. Each New Year's Day the nail was trimmed with due pomp and circumstance. It was then sent to the royal jeweller who polished it, shaped it, edged it with gold and encrusted it with diamonds. The King then presented this priceless artefact to his favourite mistress of the moment.

💰 The Baroness Angela Burdett-Coutts, a close friend of Charles Dickens, was one of the richest women of the Victorian era. Whereas most philanthropists of her time only gave money to morally uplift and inspire people – by building libraries and art galleries or offering scholarships, for example – the baroness gave to far wider and more eclectic worthy causes.

She founded a charity for the protection of the Australian Aborigine, funded drinking fountains for dogs, fed poor peasants in Turkey and bought new bells for St Paul's Cathedral.

George and Richard Cadbury, founders of the Cadbury's chocolate empire, saw themselves as having a moral and social duty towards their employees. In 1879, they built an entire village – Bournville – to house their 320 workers, and provided not only housing but also cricket and football pitches, open-air swimming pools, a concert hall and a lecture theatre. 'No man ought to be compelled to live where a rose cannot grow,' said George. In 1902, the factory became the first in Britain to have its own doctor and a works dentist was provided soon afterwards.

No matter how kind and 'enlightened' they thought themselves, they still applied a strict code of conduct to their workforce. Most workdays began with a Bible reading and some hymns in a service led by George himself. All female employees were told to have a bath at least once a week, and male and female workers were strictly segregated both in and out of work. A night-watchman was employed to guard the women's houses to ensure no hanky-panky went on. George, though, would sometimes visit their homes – but only to lead them in an impromptu hymn–singing session. Married women would not be employed because George Cadbury believed that a married woman's place was in the home. Any female employee contemplating marriage had to sit through a stern lecture on virtue from 'Governor George', before she received her wedding gift – a Bible and a carnation. There was no pub in Bournville, as both Cadbury brothers were strict teetotallers.

Fellow chocolate millionaires Joseph and Henry Rowntree

were not quite as strict. Women workers were told to wear modest black dresses which covered everything from the ankle to the throat, and girls under seventeen had to attend 'homemaking lessons'. Male apprentices were encouraged to improve themselves by doing PE and taking part in the 'Cocoa Works Debating Society'. But the Rowntrees were known for little acts of kindness towards their staff, like taking pork pies and cups of cocoa to those doing overtime. Workers recorded their own hours and were paid on trust.

They did embarrass the Rowntrees once, though, by getting drunk en masse on a works outing to Whitby. They had to be escorted back to the station by police. Works outings were off after that.

£ **What is it about chocolate manufacturers and their desire to build towns? In America, Milton Hershey made his first $1 million selling caramels, and then moved into chocolates in a big way. Within just three years he had established his very own town. Choosing a name for it proved difficult. He thought of Ulikit (You like it), Chococoa City and Qualitytells, but preferred Hersheykoko. The post office put the kibosh on that idea, however, saying that it sounded silly and they weren't going to deliver any post to a town called Hersheykoko. This was an odd attitude, because they did deliver post to Toad Suck Arkansas, Intercourse Pennsylvania, Tightwad Missouri, Pee Pee Ohio, Looneyville Texas and Superior Bottom West Virginia ...**

Anyway, I digress. Eventually Hershey decided to call the town ... Hershey. And the town, to be sure, was all his. He owned the chocolate factory. He owned the banks. He owned the ice hockey team. He

owned the zoo, the museum, the boating lake and even the cinema – where he would personally take it upon himself to censor the films. Every day he would walk out to inspect the town, and if he caught any workers playing truant from the factory he'd fire them on the spot. Hershey remained his pride and joy until he died, leaving $66 million to its future prosperity.

He left his company to the Milton Hershey School for Orphaned Boys which he had established in 1909. Nowadays the Milton Hershey School and School Trust still own the majority of his candy company, which is still thriving today.

When a hardened socialist attacked Andrew Carnegie about the redistribution of wealth, the steel tycoon asked his secretary for two numbers. The first was the value of all his assets and the second was the world's population. He divided the former by the latter and gave his critic sixteen cents, his personal share of Carnegie's net worth.

Chapter 3

A FOOL AND HIS MONEY ...

> *Gambling is a sure way of getting nothing
> for something.*
> —Wilson Mizner

Just because people have made a lot of money doesn't mean that they're necessarily going to be able to hang on to it. Some lose it faster than they can make it. Some spend it faster than it comes in. And very large numbers spend it on the most unlikely things.

For example, Henry Ford's main passion in life may have been motor cars, but running a very close second was the soya bean. He truly believed that the soya bean was the future of virtually everything. He thought that soya milk would make the cow obsolete, and wasted a small fortune trying to find a way to build an entire car out of soya beans. He even turned up at an automobile convention in a suit woven from soya fabrics. And, at the 1934 Century of Progress Fair in Chicago, his company served guests with a huge meal – all sixteen courses of which (including the coffee!) were made from soya beans.

Then there's Tommy Manville. He just spent all his money on getting married. Tommy was the heir to an industrial fortune. His trust fund stipulated that he would receive $250,000 on the day of his wedding. He got married for the first time in 1911, aged seventeen – and a further twelve times between then and 1967, when he died aged seventy-three. Each time the trust fund had to pay out the $250,000. Manville claimed that the first thing he said to a girl was 'Will you marry me?' and the next was 'How do you do?'

Most of Manville's thirteen brides were actresses and show girls. His seventh marriage was the briefest; he and his wife separated eight hours after the service. His last marriage took place in 1960 when he was sixty-six. His bride then was a waitress of just twenty-two.

It seems that many people who have made lots of money develop some very odd lifestyles …

£ According to Groucho Marx, W. C. Fields kept $50,000 worth of liquor in his attic. When asked if he knew that Prohibition was over, Fields was said to have replied, 'Yes. But it might come back.' That was typical of Fields's shrewd planning. He even kept $50,000 in bank accounts in Hitler's Germany: 'Just in case the little bastard wins.'

The first words spoken by telephone were between wealthy inventor Alexander Graham Bell and his assistant. They were, 'Watson, come here please. I want you.' Bell had just spilled battery acid down the front of his trousers and was in rather urgent need of assistance ...

💷 **French King Philip Augustus decreed that the more important you were in French society, the longer and pointier shoes you could wear. Some shoes, like the poulaine, had two-foot long tips! This caused enormous problems for the more fashion-conscious French crusader knight. At the battle of Nicopolis in 1396, the knights kept falling over their pointy shoes as they tried to run away, and had to hack their shoe tips off before they could flee to safety.**

💰. Fabulously wealthy King Boris of Bulgaria and his younger brother were both real train enthusiasts. They insisted on driving the royal train themselves – and would always have heated squabbles about who would do the driving and who would shovel the coal …

Thomas Crapper apparently followed up his invention of the one-piece pedestal flushing toilet with the world's first self-raising toilet seat. It quickly proved unpopular – not least because it tended to give people a sound spanking as they sat down …

. An illiterate Gambian villager called Dit Babini Sissoko became a multi-millionaire after persuading the Dubai Islamic Bank to lend him £150 million! Between 1995 and 1998, Mohammed Ayyoub Saleh, the bank's manager at its Dubai Headquarters, authorised 183 money transfers to Sissoko – and let Sissoko or his friends withdraw a further £50 million in cash, which they took away in black plastic bags. For some reason, the bank manager asked for no collateral, or guarantees – not even Sissoko's signature on a scrap of paper. By the time the matter came to light, Sissoko was well away and only £2 million could be clawed back.

By all accounts, Sissoko had – and is still having – a whale of a time. He's used the money to buy a small airline, a hotel business and gold mines, as well as to stay one step ahead of the frantic bank authorities. During an eighteen-month stay in Miami, the fifty-three-year-old spent $40 million on exclusive properties and cars, while donating $1.2 million to a homeless shelter.

Mohammed Ayyoub Saleh, meanwhile, has had a lot of explaining to do – and has put his strange and very costly lapse of judgement down to 'black magic'. Sissoko apparently bewitched him over dinner, and then hung a black ball on his bedroom ceiling which he claimed would allow him to watch

Saleh. He also smeared an unidentified black substance on the banker's arm which gave Sissoko black magic power over him. This is probably why he believed Sissoko when the Gambian told him that he could magic the money back into the vaults whenever Saleh needed it back.

That's the bank for me. Can anyone lend me a pointy hat and a black cat? I feel an urge to make a withdrawal coming on …

£ Pablo Picasso was probably the richest and most successful artist who ever lived. When he died in 1973 aged ninety-one, his estate was worth an estimated $1.1 billion. Towards the end of his long and successful life Picasso had virtually given up using cash at all. He was effectively drawing his own bank notes. He often paid bills by doing a little scribble or doodle which the lucky creditor could then sell for a vast sum as a genuine Picasso. It's little wonder, then, that Picasso produced an estimated 14,000 canvases and 100,000 prints and engravings during his lifetime.

£. Millionaire inventor Thomas Edison invented many great things, but it wasn't his finest hour by any means when he created the 'voice-powered sewing machine'. It worked by transforming sound waves into energy. To make it go you stuck your lips into a mouthpiece and screamed as loud as you could. The louder and longer you screamed, the longer the sewing machine worked!

£ It is now an honoured tradition in Thailand to have a vasectomy to celebrate the Thai King Bhumibol Adulyadej's birthday. The vasectomies are performed free of charge during an all-day carnival event. Incidentally, the number one hit record of all time in Thailand is an uplifting little tune called 'I'm

Vasectomised', and Thailand holds the world record for vasectomies, when fifty doctors snipped 1,119 patients in a nine–hour 'vasectathon' in 1983.

> 'To be clever enough to get all that money, one must be stupid enough to want it.'
> – G. K. Chesterton

. In 1885, future newspaper tycoon William Randolph Hearst was thrown out of Harvard for presenting each of his teachers with a chamber pot with their picture and name at the bottom …

Ted Turner may be a whiz at global media but there may be something lacking when it comes to more interpersonal communications. In 1986, he gave a speech on world peace and said, 'Imagine the Italians at war. I mean, what a joke. They didn't belong in the last war. They were sorry they were in it. They were glad to get out of it. They'd rather be involved in crime and just making wine and having a good time …'

. One American millionaire by the name of Walter Winans on his first deerstalking holiday in Scotland soon got tired of all the walking involved and decided to do it on horseback instead. Unfortunately his white horse could be seen by the deer a mile off. Determined not to be beaten he had his horse dyed black with hair dye and set off back in pursuit again. Only now, the deer could smell the dye a mile off and kept well away. The American gave up and returned home.

King Frederick William I of Prussia was obsessed with soldiers. He liked them tall. Very tall. It became

his life's work to have the world's tallest army, scouring Europe for giants to enlist. As gifts, both the Czar of Russia and the Sultan of Turkey sent him the tallest men they could find. So desperate was Frederick for big boys to join his army that he kidnapped tall monks from monasteries and strapping farm labourers as they lay sleeping at night. He even ran a sort of prototype dating agency, bringing together tall men and tall women in the hope of breeding a race of tall children for his future army. Ironically, his whole concept of an army of giants proved to be a disaster on the battlefield. They were easy targets. You couldn't miss them.

. Robert Cheeseborough, the inventor of Vaseline, ate a spoonful of it every day, believing it gave him long life. It clearly worked – as he lived to the ripe old age of ninety-six.

> Before she was famous Madonna once did a commercial – for Preparation H haemorrhoid cream.

Since Estee Lauder beauty products weren't available back in the fourth century, Queen Isabel of Bavaria concocted her own make-up – from fresh boar's brains, wolf's blood and crocodile glands.

. Cereal tycoon John Harvey Kellogg never consummated his marriage to his wife Ella. Instead, he spent their entire wedding night working on his book Plain Facts for Young and Old – a 644-page rant against the evils of sex. He spent ninety-seven pages discussing self-abuse, and pinpointed many key ways by which a self-abuser can be identified. They include acne, a love of solitude, unusual boldness, insomnia, mental confusion and smoking …

> 'A celebrity is a person who works hard all his life to become well known, then wears dark glasses to avoid being recognised.'
> – Fred Allen

£ If you were anyone in Parisian high society in the 1920s you went around on a pogo stick. The craze developed after a French explorer discovered the pogo stick being used by Borneo natives in their sacrificial dances.

💰. Back when he was still a struggling and relatively unknown painter, Francis Bacon was taken out to dinner by Lionel Bart. Bart had just had a huge commercial success with *Oliver!* and was living the high life. During dinner, Bacon was startled by Bart's behaviour. Every so often, the composer would duck under his dining table, fumble around and then reappear with a white powdery substance smeared all over his upper lip. Bacon could only stare in disbelief at Bart's brazen and clumsy behaviour. The meal finished and, as the pair were leaving, Bacon noticed that Bart had dropped a small bag of the white powder under his seat. Being pretty desperate at the time, he picked it up and hurriedly pocketed it without Bart seeing. Later that day, Bacon slipped the bag to a doorman at one of London's most exclusive nightclubs and was ushered inside along with his friends. They had just begun to enjoy themselves when the doorman rushed up and grabbed them. He had traces of the white powder on his lips and up his nose, and was having a great deal of trouble breathing as he threw them out with a tirade of abuse. The doorman's nostrils had become glued shut, because whatever Bacon thought the white powder was, it was actually some dental fixative that Lionel Bart had been using following a recent operation on his mouth ...

💰 The oil barons of Texas might have a lot more money than the Royal Family but nowhere near as much class. When Prince Charles visited Dallas he was invited to a cocktail party hosted by the city's wealthiest oil men. He was introduced by the host in the following way: 'Boys, this is the Prince of Wales. Prince of Wales, these are the boys.'

💰 **During the dark days of World War Two, Norway's exiled King Haakon came to the BBC to make a stirring speech live to his enslaved people.**

The programme started, but instead of a royal fanfare of trumpets, hundreds of thousands of Norwegians were baffled to hear a cheeky cockney chorus raucously singing 'Roll out the barrel, we'll have a barrel of fun' … followed by their King's rather confused voice. The broadcast over, the BBC held an immediate enquiry into the incident and discovered that their Sound Library was the culprit. The producer had asked for a 'fanfare'. They'd misread his order and thought he wanted a 'funfair'…

In 1989, a man out collecting bamboo shoots in a thicket on the outskirts of Tokyo found a bag containing £583,316. Strangely, he handed it in to the police. Five days later, the man was collecting bamboo shoots again in the same thicket and found a second bag, containing 100 million Yen, or £434,000. Again, he handed it in to the police, who began an intensive investigation. They discovered that the money belonged to a wealthy businessman named Kazuyasu Noguchi. He told the police that rather than pay tax on the money, he'd hidden it in the bamboo thicket and hoped that whoever picked it up would donate it to charity …

Eccentric oil billionaire H. L. Hunt gave up smoking his favourite cigars for a peculiar reason. He'd worked out that his time was worth $40,000 an hour and it was costing him too much to keep on looking for matches!

. There's no stopping progress – that is, unless you're loaded. In the 1840s, the railway was spreading throughout Britain and most people welcomed it – except the few wealthy individuals who had invested in canals. The railway threatened to make canals obsolete and worthless overnight.

One such investor was the sixth Earl of Harborough. He was threatened with losing a packet and then – to add insult to injury – the Midland Railway Company announced its intention to build its proposed Peterborough to Leicester line straight through the Earl's Stapleford Park Estate. 'Over my dead body,' said the Earl, or something like that.

At first, the railway company tried to bribe the Earl, offering him his own private waiting room at a local station, done up with appropriate luxury. They even offered him the power to flag down any passing train whenever he wanted to go anywhere. The Earl declined.

Undeterred, the railway surveyors started to sneak onto his estate at night to begin their work, and the Earl set his gamekeepers on them. There were several violent skirmishes – and then all-out war was declared. In November 1844, the railway surveyors recruited a crack team of 100 drunks, half-wits and thugs to storm the Earl's estate. But the Earl had formed his own men into a crack cavalry unit, and the battle was fierce and bloody, and raged on and off for almost two years. The Earl successfully saw off the forces of the railway before the courts became involved. They ruled in the Earl's favour, and Parliament itself passed an act in June 1846 declaring that the railway would bypass the Earl's estate. The railway line, when it was built, featured a sharp bend to avoid Stapleford Park. It became known to everyone working on the railway as 'Lord Harborough's Curve' …

During World War Two, Winston Churchill was particularly impressed by the quality of the press summaries coming out of Britain's embassy in Washington DC. He asked who had written them and was told that the author was a Mr I. Berlin – a scholar named Isaiah Berlin.

Shortly afterwards, hearing that Berlin was in London,

Churchill invited him to a lunch party. By all accounts everything went well until Churchill asked Berlin for his views on the outcome of the war and President Rooservelt's chances in the forthcoming elections. Everyone present was stunned as Berlin gave a rambling and ill-informed series of guesses, eventually confessing that he really didn't know much about that sort of stuff. It gradually dawned on Churchill that he'd invited the wrong I. Berlin to lunch. The man sitting next to him was actually Irving Berlin, composer of 'White Christmas' ...

Incidentally, Winston was a man who, between winning wars, clearly spent a lot of time at the dinner table. The anecdotes that have emerged from his many meals are legendary. At a Blenheim Palace dinner party, he once found himself seated near the millionaire Waldorf Astor and his wife Nancy. Nancy argued with Churchill on every topic that came up, and finally said, 'If I were married to you, I'd put poison in your coffee.'

Churchill calmly replied: 'Nancy, if I were married to you I'd drink it.'

The Reverend Sylvester Graham believed that the root cause of insanity was eating mustard or tomato ketchup. He also believed that eating meat was the cause of all male beastliness. To help people escape these woes, he established a chain of Graham boarding houses which made him exceedingly rich. Thousands lived there, safe from the perils of meat, mustard and ketchup ...

. Uri Geller's real wealth doesn't come from public displays of his psychic talents, but from his highly successful (but little publicised) ability to prospect for oil and valuable minerals. Companies the world over have employed his psychic abilities – and it seems to work. Uri starts by dowsing with a map, and then flies over any likely area in a small plane, holding his hand out of the window to 'feel' the deposits under the ground.

However he once threw £17,000 worth of winnings from a casino out of the window of his limousine – because he felt he had abused his powers.

In 1974, a Swedish woman filed a paternity suit against Uri. He'd never met her, let alone slept with her, but she claimed that his mental powers had bent her contraceptive coil and caused her to get pregnant …

And finally, when he wasn't promoting the cause of the soya bean, car manufacturer Henry Ford spent a lot of time in court, dealing with all sorts of law suits. In 1919 Henry found himself answering general knowledge questions – quiz show style – in a Chicago court, to prove he wasn't stupid. Three years before, a journalist on the *Chicago Tribune* had made disparaging remarks about Ford, calling him among other things 'ignorant' and 'an anarchist'.

Henry Ford's lawyer, Alfred Lucking, immediately filed a million-dollar law suit – but made a fundamental error. Of course Henry Ford wasn't an anarchist. If Lucking had gone to court on that, he would have won easily. Instead, he sued on the grounds that Henry Ford was not ignorant – and put his client in a world of trouble. Ford, after all, was the man who had said 'history is more or less bunk' and prided himself on not being academic. When the trial came to court, the *Chicago Tribune*'s lawyer, Elliot Stevenson, wiped the floor with Ford by acting as a quizmaster and bombarding him with general knowledge questions! When asked when the American Revolution had taken place, Ford answered 1812. He also thought that 'chilli con carne' was a large mobile army and incorrectly identified famous American traitor Benedict Arnold as a writer. Not surprisingly, Henry Ford won just six cents compensation …

Chapter 4

HOW TO LOSE FRIENDS AND INFLUENCE PEOPLE

'
Being rich means you can buy what you want, do what you want, and not give a damn.
– J. P. Morgan
'

There is no doubt that some people who earn a lot of money really don't deserve it. Nobody can condone their behaviour, nobody has a good word to say for them – but they remain sickeningly wealthy.

For example, Emperor Bokassa Ist of the Central African Republic spent one third of his country's entire annual income on his coronation in 1977. The average annual salary at the time was £16.50, but a disgraceful £1.5 million alone was spent on perfumed French-style wigs for his courtiers, and his queen wore a dress studded with three quarters of a million pearls. Queen Elizabeth, although invited, made her excuses and stayed away – which is probably just as well as it is strongly rumoured that Bokassa's political prisoners, of whom there were a large number, were served up as boeuf bourguignon during the banquet that followed ...

The name Leona Helmsley might not be familiar to you but her famous saying 'We don't pay taxes. Only the little people pay taxes' probably is. This quote was thrown back in her face when she stood trial in 1989 on five counts of tax evasion, filing false returns and conspiracy to defraud the tax man. How much tax did she owe? Just $1.7 million.

Leona and her husband Harry were hotel magnates, millionaires many times over, owning twenty-six hotels, including the prestigious Park Lane Hotel in Manhattan. She saw herself as the queen of her empire and lived accordingly, owning a twenty-eight bedroom Connecticut mansion and travelling around in her personal Boeing 727.

Although successful, her management style could be described as 'strong' (if you're being polite) or 'unreasonably aggressive and dictatorial' (if the truth is known). Her attention to detail was fastidious – as employees learned to their cost. Leona fired one waiter on the spot when she noticed one of his fingernails was dirty. Another was given his marching orders because his hand trembled slightly when he served her a glass of wine. She used to make on-the-spot inspections of random rooms and once sacked a maid for leaving unadjusted a lampshade that was not quite straight.

When she wasn't running her empire or firing staff, Leona used to relax in her penthouse swimming pool. A liveried valet stood at one end of the pool holding a solid silver platter of shrimps. As she completed a lap she would clap her hands and shout out, 'Feed the fishy!' – at which point a shrimp would be placed delicately in her mouth.

Leona was convicted of her tax frauds and imprisoned in 1992 aged seventy-one. After her trial, one of the jurors summed up the jury's feelings, claiming: 'We did it for the little people.'

P.S. As an aside, Helmsley was paroled in 1993 and ordered to carry out 250 hours of community service, wrapping gifts and stuffing envelopes for charity. Two years later her employees complained that their boss was forcing them to do the work instead of her – in between their regular duties. The judge was not impressed and added an extra 150 hours of community service on to her sentence.

The American railroad tycoon Jay Gould was once approached by the minister of his church and asked where he might invest $30,000 of his life savings. The millionaire suggested that a good investment was in the stock offered by the Missouri Pacific Railroad. Sworn to secrecy, the clergyman followed this advice. A few months later, however, the stock lost most of its value and, kindly, Gould reimbursed the minister. The minister then owned up to the tycoon that he had failed to keep the secret and had in fact passed the investment tip to a great many members of his congregation.

Gould was delighted. He told the minister, 'I assumed you would. You see, they were the ones I was after.'

They can be real bastards sometimes, these millionaires. Lounging around his London club one day in 1907, the American banker John Pierpont Morgan decided to have a wager with one Lord Lonsdale. The wager started out as to whether a chap could walk around the world – but then things got strange. Morgan desperately wanted to know if it was possible to walk around the world with a knight's helmet over your head while pushing a pram.

Well, you would, wouldn't you?

Then it got even stranger. Morgan wanted to know if it could be done with only £1 in your pocket and one spare pair of underpants. (I suspect alcohol was involved by this point.) Morgan made two further conditions on the wager: the walker must finance his journey only by selling postcards of himself and – somewhere along the way – he must get married without ever revealing his masked face to his bride.

So desperate were the two millionaires to know if this was possible that they offered a prize of around £20,000 to anyone who could do it. Step forward Harry Bensley, an eighteen-year-old from Thetford who decided to take the two men up on the challenge.

Harry started his epic journey at Trafalgar Square on New Year's Day 1908, but only got as far as Kent before being arrested. Selling postcards without a hawker's licence was a criminal offence and Harry found himself hauled up before Bexleyheath Court. They sportingly allowed him to keep his helmet on throughout the trial, but fined him two and sixpence.

Harry had his second stroke of misfortune shortly afterwards when, setting off again, he decided to go west instead of east. Instead of crossing Europe first, he elected to walk across Ireland, gain passage to America and cross that vast continent. For six years he walked, always with his helmet on, pushing the pram. He crossed America, shipped himself out to Japan, then China. He walked across India, across Persia and up through Turkey to the Balkans. Along the way, over 200 women proposed to him, but he never accepted. Now, arriving in Italy, he was at last on the home stretch. Europe beckoned.

And then World War One broke out, right in his path.

That was it. Back home in London, Morgan decided to call the wager off. Poor Harry tossed his helmet and pram away in disgust and caught the first boat for England.

The mean-spirited Morgan gave Harry £4,000 for his trouble, but Harry was so annoyed that he gave the entire sum to charity. Then he promptly signed up with the British Army and went off to fight in France. You'll be pleased to learn that he survived the war – he deserved that much luck – and went on to become a local councillor in Wivenhoe, Essex, before retiring to Brighton and taking his final journey in 1970.

£ When Joan Crawford became a hugely successful film star, rumours started to emerge that she'd made hard-core porno movies in her teens. To prevent the press discovering any firm evidence, Crawford took it upon herself personally to make sure every last print

was destroyed – and paid a private detective $100,000 to track them all down. Finally, only one copy was left – but it belonged to a collector who refused to part with it at any price. Crawford needn't have worried. A few weeks after he turned down her offer, his house burned to the ground and both he and the film perished in the flames …

On 20 July 1996, over 6,000 sick individuals put their money on 8-0-0 in the Connecticut daily state lottery. They chose the number because 800 was the flight number of the TWA Jumbo that had crashed off Long Island the week before. The number hit – and the lottery had to pay out over $1 million in winnings.

. Russell Sage is widely regarded as America's answer to Scrooge. He built up a personal fortune of some $70 million, largely through investments and moneylending, but refused to wear anything more extravagant than a $4 secondhand suit. Business lunches with Sage were dreaded – not least because all the old skinflint would offer his guests was an apple. Sage's meanness was only matched by his cowardice. In 1891, a man walked into Sage's offices with dynamite strapped to him and threatened to blow him up unless he was given £1,200,000. Sage's first response was to grab the nearest of his employees and hide behind him. The bomb went off, killing the robber and badly injuring the employee. Sage survived, but steadfastly refused to pay his employee even one cent in compensation!

Equally mean – perhaps even meaner – was George Washington, America's first millionaire. This was partly due to the fact that he married the richest widow in the state of Virginia, and partly because he was superb at keeping accounts, was a bit of a wide boy, and as tight as a duck's derrière to boot.

He refused a salary to lead the Revolutionary Army during the American War of Independence. 'I'll just take expenses', he said patriotically. However, from 1775–1793, his expenses came to almost half a million dollars – a nice little earner. When Washington got elected as the country's first President, he was again offered a salary and again turned it down saying that he was a loyal American and would only claim his expenses. However, by now America had got wise to Washington's 'expenses' and absolutely insisted he took an annual salary of $25,000 instead …

It didn't matter to Washington, who had his fingers in a lot of pies. He was America's first mule breeder and had a very profitable sideline growing hemp – or marijuana. In fact, he imported plants and seeds into America from all over the world.

Washington's meanness was also legendary. He hired a lady named Mary Firth to do his laundry but had it stipulated that under the terms of the agreement she had to pay for the soap.

People thought he always looked resolute and determined with his jaw clenched tight – but that was merely due to the fact that he was too tight to pay for a better fitting set of dentures.

> **'Hollywood is a place where they'll pay you a thousand dollars for a kiss and fifty cents for your soul.'**
> **– Marilyn Monroe**

. When Peter the Great of Russia discovered that his wife had taken a lover, he exacted a terrible revenge. He had the lover decapitated and the severed head pickled in a jar of alcohol. The jar was then placed in a prominent place in the Queen's bedroom …

One morning, the owners of the London and Greenwich Railway Company were somewhat taken aback by a letter they received. It said simply:

> *Sirs,*
>
> *I am anxious to witness a train smash. If you will allow two of your engines to collide head on at full speed, I will contribute a sum of £10,000 to your funds.'*
>
> *Waterford.*

Naturally, the railway executives ignored the letter, assuming the author was mad. They weren't far wrong.

Henry de la Poor Beresford, the third Marquis of Waterford, was mad – and bad. They even called him 'the Mad Marquis'. Too much free time – and too much money – made him a thoroughly debauched individual. When he wasn't hunting and killing any defenceless creature unwise enough to cross his path, he and his gang of cronies from Lord Rokesby's Club would go in search of human prey to beat up and humiliate, safe in the notion that they could easily afford any fine – or bribe. The Marquis was unceremoniously ejected from America after he and his chums sailed to New York on a whim, smashed two street lamps and some windows in Manhattan and then attacked and stripped a startled American citizen and a night watchman who came to help. Two years later, he and his chums pulled the same stunt in Norway, and a watchman there who had the temerity to defend himself as the English noblemen tried to strip him naked actually found himself in court on assault charges. Back home, the Marquis amused himself by bravura displays of indoor showjumping, vandalising road signs and amassing a collection of thousands of door knobs and knockers stolen from people's houses at night. For a laugh he would sneak a donkey into a nearby inn and smuggle it into bed with an unsuspecting guest.

Before doing the world a favour by breaking his neck in a riding accident while out hunting, the Marquis actually did contribute something to British culture that survives to this day. One night in April 1837, he and his drunken gang of Hooray Henrys descended on his local town of Melton Mowbray in Leicestershire armed with several drums of red paint. When the townsfolk awoke in the morning, they emerged to find many of the town's most prominent buildings – and the night watchman himself – smeared and spattered with fresh paint from door to roof. They weren't best amused – but the English language ended up with a new phrase – 'to paint the town red'...

£ Hollywood mogul Sam Goldwyn once instructed his publicist Arthur L. Mayer to train seventy parrots to squawk the title of Mae West's new film *It Ain't No Sin*. Against all odds Mayer achieved it and had all seventy parrots yelling the title loud and clear. Then, on a whim, Goldwyn changed the name of the film to *I'm No Angel*. Mayer quit on the spot.

Pere Gourier was an extremely wealthy landowner in eighteenth-century France who also had a strange hobby. He murdered people – but in a bizarre and legal way – by getting his victims to eat themselves to death.

Gourier would choose his victim, befriend them, then invite them to a weekly series of huge and richly-cooked meals and insist on paying the bill. After two or three months of this hospitality the victim would die, usually of a heart attack. Gourier met his comeuppance when he chose as his victim a man named Ameline. The pair of them began eating in the finest restaurants in Paris but, tipped off by a waiter who suspected Gourier's motives, Ameline used to fast between meals.

After twelve months, Gourier could not understand how his latest victim had survived for so long eating rich meal after rich meal – and it made him even more determined to succeed in killing him. After two years of matching Ameline plate for plate the killer finally met his end as they were both eating an enormous steak, matching each other bite for bite. Both men were in the middle of their fourteenth slice when Gourier sat bolt upright, turned white then slumped down head first into his plate, having had a fatal heart attack.

After the ladies had retired after a rather magnificent banquet at Dunraven Castle, the wealthy host, Lord Turberville, commented to a gentleman present that the woman who had been seated on his right during dinner was possibly the ugliest woman he had ever seen. The guest replied, 'I am sorry you found my wife so unattractive.' Trying to excuse his remark, Lord Turberville then flustered, 'I beg your pardon, sir. I meant to say the woman on my left.' The same man then told him, 'Well, that lady, sir, happens to be my sister.'

'Your sister, eh?' said the peer. Then, after a deathly silence, added, 'Well, in that case, I must admit that I have never seen such an ugly family in my entire life!'

. Starting out as a humble sergeant, 'Big Daddy' Idi Amin rose to be Uganda's el supremo in 1971 and set new records for terror and corruption, even for a country with such a terrible history – and even though the *Daily Mirror* had described him as 'a thoroughly nice man … as gentle as a lamb', and the *Financial Times* had summed him up as 'Without doubt, a benevolent, honest, dedicated and hardworking man.'

Amin killed 300,000 fellow Ugandans and enjoyed eating those who had particularly displeased him. Yet he was terrified of a tortoise said to be wandering Uganda fermenting rebellion, and personally asked Emperor Hirohito of Japan for a squadron of kamikaze planes to use against the tortoise. He also personally wrote to wish ex-president Nixon a speedy recovery from Watergate and volunteered to take over the running of the Commonwealth. One of his proudest boasts was: 'Uganda has among the best prisons in the world and people from many countries are eager to visit them' …

THE SCREAM
MUNCH

£ **In 1975 the rock band Led Zeppelin held a press conference in a Copenhagen Art Gallery. A rock critic started talking to drummer John Bonham about a valuable painting on display, rather than talking about the band's new album. Bonham was completely disinterested. When the critic didn't get the hint, Bonham went over to the painting, took it off the wall**

and broke it over the critic's head. Bonham then asked him, 'Are there any other paintings you'd like me to critique tonight?'

. One of the greatest religious charlatans of this century – and there are plenty to choose from – was Father Divine. He claimed that God had despatched him to Earth thousands of years ago to preach peace, celibacy and honesty. Actually he was born plain George Baker in Rockville, Maryland, in 1879, and he was anything but honest – or celibate.

After learning a few tricks of the trade from black churches at the turn of the century, Father Divine went into business for himself, preaching first in the streets of Harlem. His sermons were deliberately meant to sound knowledgeable but actually meant nothing. 'God is not only personified and materialised,' he taught, 'he is repersonified and rematerialised. He rematerialised and he rematerialises. He rematerialates and he is rematerialisatable. He repersonificates and he repersonificates!'

More impressive than his message was Father Divine's promise of eternal life. In 1919 he set up a commune, modestly called 'Heaven', on Long Island and promised that no one who lived there with him would ever die. True to his word, they didn't. At the first sign of any life-threatening illness, Father Divine would have them removed. Everyone who lived there went out to work and paid Divine a tithe. At first, Divine's 'Kingdom of Peace' movement was praised because it encouraged racial equality, but the head of the Universal Negro Improvement Association soon smelled a rat, calling the organisation 'a colossal racket'.

This didn't deter Father Divine from attracting literally millions of members world-wide – including some very important people, like a millionaire who left Divine his entire $10 million estate.

The church preached purity of body and mind. No sex.
No drink. No cigarettes. No swearing. Followers couldn't
wear make-up, accept presents or go to see movies. The word
'hello' was banned within the movement because it contained
the word 'hell' within it. Female followers would wear a large V
on their sweaters which stood for 'Virgin', and took on new
names like 'Miss Charity' and 'Holy Quietness'.

Evidently, $500 silk suits and limousines were not banned,
as Father Divine lived in them.

Despite all this, Father Divine was sued on a number of
occasions by jealous husbands as the podgy little man, who
stood about 5′ 2″ tall, allegedly slept with as many of his female
followers as he could lay his hands on – claiming that he was
only 'bringing their carnal desires to the surface so that he could
eliminate them'.

Nice work if you can get it …

**In 1846, a young American inventor called Elias
Howe invented the first sewing machine. He thought
it would make him his fortune, but nobody he talked
to seemed remotely interested. After banging his
head against a brick wall for years, Elias had a nervous
breakdown and emigrated to England to see if the
English would be more receptive to his idea. They
weren't. After two years, Elias finally gave up trying to
sell his invention and returned home. He had no
money for a ticket, so he worked his passage across
the Atlantic on a merchant ship.**

**Imagine his reaction when he arrived back in
Boston to find that the sewing machine was all the
rage – and that everyone was singing the praises of its
inventor, one Isaac Singer. Singer had stolen Howe's
patent lock, stock and barrel. Elias took him to court,**

but the fight took years. Singer could afford to buy the best lawyers with all the money he was making from Elias's invention. Happily, justice prevailed and, eventually, Howe did win a royalty on every sewing machine sold, but his name is now largely forgotten while the name Singer is still synonymous with sewing machines.

. As the Rajah of Drangadhara went off to war, his eight wives watched from the palace roof. From there they could see the battle and the Royal Standard flying, which meant that their husband was still alive on the field of battle. By tradition, the standard was only ever lowered if the Rajah fell. However, the flagbearer was suddenly caught short and laid the standard down for a moment to take a quick pee in some bushes. Seeing the standard go down, the eight wives immediately assumed that their husband was dead – and seven of them threw themselves off the palace roof to their deaths, as the ancient tradition of suttee demanded.

When the Rajah returned from the field, he was far more upset that one of his wives had failed to jump than he was about the other seven who had died in error, and ordered the eighth wife to jump to her death as well …

Sultan Osman II of Turkey (1603–1622) had more money than he knew what to do with and he soon got bored. Trying to liven his life up a bit he took up archery – using his own servants as live targets.

Despite her immortalisation as a heroine in the movie, Eva Peron started out as a child prostitute. Later in life she went to bed with Aristotle Onassis a year after she became the first lady of Argentina. She came away clutching a cheque for $10,000 'for her favourite charity'.

'Evita' made her fortune from personally robbing Argentina's state-run charities of every penny she could grab. Peron's third wife, Isabel, was also convicted in 1978 of stealing $8 million from a state-run charity.

. Emil Savundra's employees called him 'Caesar' behind his back, because he ran his business like a tyrant and lived a life of utter luxury and decadence. The fat little man from Ceylon arrived in Britain in the 1960s, having failed in business in China, Ghana and Belgium. Failed ventures had left him almost broke, but he had just enough cash reserves left to start his own insurance business called Fire, Auto & Marine. The company was an immediate success, because it offered car insurance at half the rates other companies were charging. If it sounded too good to be true, it was. Savundra's business plan relied on the company expanding forever, with the new money being used to settle old claims.

It was a time bomb waiting to go off – but Savundra didn't seem to care. He lived a life of luxury in Mayfair, had many mistresses despite being married, and mixed with Britain's elite at all the best social functions. 'I am God's own lounge lizard,' he boasted.

Two years later, claims against Fire, Auto & Marine finally exceeded its income. To prevent the British Government closing him down, Savundra created fake accounts that simply allowed the problem to keep getting worse. By 1966, 400,000 people in Britain had unpaid claims with his company. Fire, Auto & Marine collapsed and Savundra fled to Switzerland, but returned to the UK a year later and actually lived on the dole while hatching new money-making schemes. When David Frost invited him onto his TV show, Savundra's towering ego could not decline. Under the studio lights, Frost crucified the swindler in front of an audience packed with those who had been ripped off by his insurance company. Savundra revealed himself to be totally heartless and unsympathetic. Asked to sum up what had happened, he cavalierly replied, 'But of course, it was all fun ...' When confronted by two widows who had received no compensation, he brazenly sneered at them, saying, 'I have no legal or moral responsibility!' Then, as the studio audience became even more irate, Savundra snapped, 'I do not want to cross swords with peasants!' That was it. Savundra had to be escorted from the studio under police escort for his own protection.

Eventually, Savundra was taking to court for fraud and sentenced to eight years in jail, where he had plenty of time to hatch new crackpot schemes. On his release, the first thing he did was to contact the American Government and offer them the chance to site strategic nuclear missiles on his wife's estate in Ceylon. In return, he wanted the US Government to pay him $200 million and arrange for him to become King of Ceylon. They never replied, and Savundra died, penniless, in 1976.

> 'We must believe in luck. How else can we explain the success of those we don't like?'
> — Jean Cocteau

'A banker is a fellow who lends you his umbrella when the sun is shining and wants it back the minute it begins to rain.'
— Mark Twain

> 'If you want to know what God thinks about money, just look at the people He gives it to.'
> — Old Irish Saying

Chapter 5

ILL GOTTEN GAINS

‘
Behind every fortune there is a crime.
– Balzac
’

The old adage that crime doesn't pay isn't necessarily always true. In fact, the reality is that thousands of men and women have become very very rich indeed from what might euphemistically be called confidence tricks, but more accurately called fraud. And, in many cases, far from the crime not paying, they've lived very happily ever after indeed, thank you, on the proceeds of their illegal activities.

The hit film *The Sting* was inspired by the actions of a real con man, Joseph Weil, who is thought to be the greatest con man ever to operate in America. Weil was the master of a whole range of lucrative scams, but his most audacious was undoubtedly the ‘fake bank con’.

He rented an old bank's premises in Muncie, Indiana, then printed convincing documents, hired phoney tellers and customers and filled money bags with worthless lead coins. By putting on this charade he was able to convince wealthy customers that he ran a legitimate bank. When enough people had deposited large amounts with him he simply closed the bank and moved on.

It's estimated that in the early 1900s Weil's various scams earned him over $6 million.

Joshua Tatum, a deaf nineteenth-century counterfeiter, made a fortune from turning several thousand nickels (five-cent pieces) into $5 gold coins, therefore increasing their value one hundred times. The method was ingenious. It started when he noticed that the nickels (which were the same size as the gold five-dollar coins) had the Roman numeral 'V' engraved on them, representing five. There was no other wording to indicate whether this was five cents – or any other denomination.

Tatum hired a jeweller to gold-plate the coins and mill the edges and then went from store to store making five-cent purchases. Indicating that he was stone-deaf, he accepted the $4.95 change passed to him without uttering a word. Soon he had amassed a large sum of money.

It was inevitable that he would be arrested but at the trial he was acquitted. The reason was that Tatum had never attempted to purchase more than five cents' worth of goods with any of the coins – and he hadn't actually asked for the change. It had just been given to him across the counter.

After the trial the US mint made it clear that a nickel was worth five cents – not five anything else – and it became a federal offence to deface or alter US currency.

Before he became a wealthy actor David Niven and his friend Doug Hertz used to employ an ingenious trick to get cheap meals. The scam worked liked this: Niven would enter a busy restaurant in New York where he would order something light, like a coffee and a doughnut and just sit, reading a newspaper. A few minutes later Hertz would enter and, acting like a complete stranger, ask Niven if he could share his table. Hertz would then order steak with all the trimmings. Both men would ignore each other and finish their meal, and ask for their respective bills. Once these were both on the table Niven would visit the washroom while Hertz went to pay – but he would pay Niven's bill as if it were his own.

When Niven returned he would find that 'his' bill was for steak – when all he had eaten was a coffee and a doughnut. Niven would then complain to the manager that he'd been the victim of a trick. By this time, Hertz had long gone and all the manager could do was issue Niven with a correct bill. They couldn't make him pay for the steak as he hadn't actually eaten it.

Niven would settle his bill then leave, only to meet up again with Hertz at another restaurant. This time, it would be Niven's turn to order the steak …

In his prime, Howard Hughes was so wealthy and so well connected that he could buy and sell politicians on a whim – and even influence presidents. It's reckoned he paid over $1 million a year as backhanders to politicians at both local and national government level. He even tried to pay off President Johnson to stop his testing nuclear weapons in the Nevada desert because he was afraid these would put off visitors to his Las Vegas hotels. Perhaps the most sinister charge levelled against Hughes is that he tried to bribe Johnson to prolong the Vietnam War. He was making so much money from his company's military contracts to supply missiles and electronic weaponry that an early cease-fire would seriously hurt his financial empire.

In the 1970s, the publishing world was rocked after a best-selling autobiography of Hughes turned out to be a complete hoax. American publishing house McGraw-Hill had believed Clifford Irving when he approached them with the news that the legendary recluse had chosen him to ghostwrite his biography. Proudly, the publishers announced that Hughes had chosen Irving 'because of his sympathy, discernment, discretion and … his integrity as a human being'.

In fact, the 1,200-page manuscript was a complete fabrication, invented by Irving and his friend Richard Suskind. Almost everyone was fooled. Even people who knew Hughes said the manuscript had to be genuine. To back up his claims, Irving produced over twenty different letters and contracts which he said were in Hughes's own handwriting. In fact, they'd been written by another associate who had never even seen a sample of Hughes's real handwriting. Despite this, five of the best handwriting analysts in America vouched that the letters were written by Hughes. When word of the book got out, Hughes broke his decades-long silence with a furious phone call denying ever having met Irving.

Irving was further caught out when his wife was exposed as having a Swiss bank account in the name of H. Hughes. Despite returning what was left of the $765,000 the publishers had paid him, Irving was convicted and sent to jail for seventeen months.

Ironically, fears about what Hughes might have revealed in the fake autobiography eventually led Richard Nixon to authorise the Watergate break-in …

£ The great funerals of the Pharaohs, such as Tutankhamun, almost bankrupted the Egyptian nation because so much gold, silver and semi-precious jewels were buried with the dead Pharaoh that there

was little left to go around. It was only the tomb robbers who dug it all up again and fed it back into the economy that kept Egypt solvent!

Oscar Merril Hartzell became a millionaire by swindling over 70,000 people. The son of an American farmer, he claimed to be working for a descendent of the illegitimate son of Sir Francis Drake (whose mother was none other than Queen Elizabeth I), who was rightful heir to an estate now worth a staggering $22 billion! Only he didn't have the money to fight the case, so Hartzell had been authorised to contact everyone named Drake and invite them to 'invest' in the court case. He promised them a guaranteed return of $500 for every dollar invested. Using a network of agents, Hartzell contacted thousands of people called Drake and the money for the fictitious court case started rolling in. All were sworn to the strictest secrecy and were told they would forfeit their share if they breathed a word to anyone else about what was going on.

Hartzell kept fleecing his victims for eleven years, weaving intricate stories about secret agents plotting his death and ongoing hush-hush negotiations with the British Treasury and the Monarchy itself before he was eventually arrested for fraud. The arrest, he claimed, was a plot by the British Secret Service to stop his client taking billions of pounds from the British Treasury. Another $350,000 rolled in from furious investors to pay for Hartzell's legal fees. It failed to save him from a ten-year sentence for fraud – but to their dying day many investors refused to believe it was all a hoax and remained convinced that they had been cheated out of their rightful inheritance by a British Government conspiracy.

Mohamed al Fayed was a big hit when he visited America. 'Call me Mo!' he told everyone jovially, while spending freely on his House of Fraser account. He even posed with the pop group Duran Duran while on their American tour. A freelance photographer took some snaps of them together and posted them off to Harrods, with a little note saying, *'Mo – here are a couple of prints from the Duran tour. Hope you like them. Dennis.'*

Back in London, Mohamed al Fayed most certainly didn't like them. Firstly, he had never been called 'Mo' by anyone in his life. Ever. Secondly, he had no idea who that was in the pictures standing next to Simon le Bon, but it most certainly wasn't him. Al Fayed spent half a million dollars hunting down the impostor – who turned out to be an ex-merchant seaman called Mohammed Yehia Saed – while the impostor ran up even more expenses and continued charging them to the House of Fraser. Eventually, the fake 'Mo' was tracked down to a hotel in New Orleans, by which time he was also wanted by police in Georgia, California, Virginia and Ontario ...

Agathocles was the wealthy ruler of Syracuse, murdered in 289BC by a grandson who couldn't wait for his inheritance. The way he was killed was ingenious and chilling. Knowing that his grandfather used to clean his teeth with his quill pen, the grandson arranged for a small amount of paralysis poison to be added to the ink. Sure enough, shortly after Agathocles cleaned his teeth he collapsed, unable to move a muscle or speak. He was left this way – apparently dead – until his funeral and eventual cremation. As Agathocles entered the flames he was still fully conscious, but incapable of speech or movement, and therefore unable to signal that he was in fact still alive ...

An equally ingenious trick was used to kill the Emperor Britannicus, one of the sons of Claudius. He was poisoned by Nero, his main rival for the Imperial throne, who used a cunning plan. Britannicus was served a hot drink and, as ever, his food taster tried it first. This was free of poison, but too hot for Britannicus to drink. He immediately cried out for cold water – and it was to this that the poison had been added ...

£ South America is notorious for the number of millionaires it has created through drug smuggling. One Brazilian, however, became a millionaire by smuggling ... playing cards! It is illegal to import playing cards into Brazil because it has its own playing card industry and the government is keen to protect it. However, Brazilian cards are notoriously tatty and flimsy, and everyone prefers imported cards, which consequently attract a premium price.

The scam was ingenious. The smuggler imported a million packs of playing cards into Brazil – all of which had the ace of spades missing. At the same time, he legally imported a million ace of spades cards, saying they were going to be turned into drinks coasters. As he expected, the government seized the million packs of playing cards. Normally, they would have burned them, but because the ace of spades was missing from each pack the government considered them completely useless and instead put them up for auction.

The smuggler attended the auction, posing as a waste paper dealer, and bought back his cards for a tiny sum, quite legally. He then reinstated the aces in the decks and sold them for $4 each!

Fed up with being poor, in March 1967 a Nigerian labourer on a building site in Lagos decided to make himself a multi-millionaire at a stroke. On receiving his pay cheque for £9.20, he took a pen and crudely changed it to £697,000,090.20. Sad to say, his ruse was spotted the moment he tried to cash the cheque and he was done for fraud.

Similarly, Vincenzo Peruggia went from humble museum attendant to multimillionaire in an instant when he cut the Mona Lisa out of its frame and smuggled it out of the Louvre one day in 1911. Staff didn't even notice it was missing until a visitor asked where it was. The painting, which was then valued at £5 million but today is estimated to be worth well over £100 million, stayed hidden away in the false bottom of a trunk in his room for two years, during which time more Parisians came to gaze at the empty space on the wall where the painting had been than had bothered to look at it when it had been there. During that time, at least six gullible Americans were sold the 'Mona Lisa' for as little as $30,000 each. Of course they were fakes.

When Vincenzo himself tried to sell the painting for just $95,000 he was arrested. At his trial in Florence, where the painting was recovered, Vincenzo desperately claimed that his real motive had been to recover the great art treasure for Italy. The judge swallowed it and gave him a particularly lenient sentence ...

Incidentally, the painter of the Mona Lisa, Leonardo da Vinci, was paid 4,000 gold florins for the work by Francis I of France, who hung the painting in a bathroom. Since, like most royalty of that time, Francis hardly ever went near the bathroom you can tell how impressed he was by it. Da Vinci was once described by friends as 'the most beautiful man who ever lived'. In recent years, it's claimed that it's been scientifically proven that the Mona Lisa is really Leonardo himself in drag! That explains the enigmatic smile ...

. In 1675, a British highwayman named Thomas Blood became a millionaire for all of twenty minutes or so when he stole the Crown Jewels from the royal treasure room of the Tower of London. Guards seized him before he could escape the Tower and it looked as if Blood was, quite literally, for the chop. However, King Charles II, it is said, was so taken by the highwayman's sheer audacity that he commuted the death sentence and instead awarded Blood an annual pension of £300 a year for the rest of his life. However, others have alleged that the King – always short of a bob or two – had been the

mastermind behind the plan to snatch the Crown Jewels and was just buying his co-conspirator's silence …

£ Can you remember the names of everyone you've ever been pally with? Neither can I, and that's exactly what two Taiwanese con artists were banking on when they hatched an ingenious scheme. They sent out 10,000 invitations to wealthy Taiwanese residents, inviting them to a wedding. Of course, the recipients didn't recognise the names of the couple getting married and, in their embarrassment, declined the invitation but sent wedding gifts instead. The con men netted a small fortune in cheques and household appliances. Even the mayor of Tai Pai was conned into sending valuable antique Chinese calligraphy scrolls as a gift.

Sheikh Shakhbut, the former ruler of Abu Dhabi, earned his country a fortune in oil revenues, but his countrymen couldn't understand why they did not enjoy much of this wealth. The unrest led to the Sheikh being deposed. When the Royal residency was inspected it was discovered that the treasury had only seen a small amount of the oil income – most of it had been hoarded in Shakhbut's royal bedroom.

Currency had been hidden away in closets, wardrobes, in the mattress, the dresser and under the bed. It was impossible to tell how much money had been taken out of the economy in this way. And at least $2 million had been eaten by rats.

When Count Von Attems arrived in Sydney in 1868, Australian Society flocked to him. Desperate for some genuine European class and breeding, they feted him wherever he went. He took the best hotels, threw lavish parties and his new friends quite happily cashed cheques for him to the tune of some £60,000. Before he returned to Europe, he threw one final lavish party to end all parties, where he remarked that he was only sorry that he hadn't been able to meet the new governor of Queensland, an old friend of his.

Von Attems set sail for Europe, and when the governor of Queensland arrived in Sydney the well-to-do of the city were only too quick to show him pictures of them posing next to his good friend. The governor took one look at the pictures and told them, 'That's not Count Von Attems. That's his valet!'

The valet was later arrested in Europe for his audacious fraud and sentenced to twenty-two years in prison.

In his day, Charles Morse swindled tens of millions of dollars out of America's rich and poor. He was only caught once at the age of fifty and sentenced to fifteen years in jail. Two years later, government doctors reported that Morse had Bright's Disease and was dying. He was pardoned and set free, then proceeded to live for another thirty years. He had faked the symptoms of the disease by drinking liquid soaps ...

> **The world's greatest jewel theft took place in 1980 when jewels valued at $16 million were stolen from the bedroom of Prince Abdul Aziz bin Ahmed Al-Thani's villa in Cannes.**

Karen Bowen met the man of her dreams one night at a Windsor night club. He was tall, dark, handsome and a millionaire. He swept her off her feet and took her back to his sumptuous home, where they romped in his luxury whirlpool bath and on his king-sized bed.

When she awoke the next morning he had gone. Staring

down at her was an estate agent with two clients she'd brought
to view the vacant house ...

Philip Arnold and John Slack were old, down on their luck
prospectors who hit upon a get rich scheme in the 1870s.
They invested their life savings in $30,000 worth of diamonds
which they then scattered around some worthless land they
owned in Wyoming.

When independent witnesses confirmed the discovery of
these stones they managed to convince the Bank of California
that they had found a diamond field. Banker William Ralston,
sensing a bargain, quickly bought the land from them for
$700,000 – a fortune in those days – thinking he'd struck the
deal of the century.

In 1990, an American tabloid printed the startling headline
'World's Oldest Newspaper Carrier, 101, Quits Because She's
Pregnant'. The story purported to be about an old but still very
frisky Australian lady who had been made pregnant by a
millionaire on her paper round. Of course it was all rubbish,
but the tabloid had used a photograph of a real person to
accompany the story. Her name was Nellie Mitchell. She was
ninety–six, lived in America and was most definitely not
amused to have friends and neighbours ask her when the baby
was due. Nellie sued for invasion of privacy and extreme
emotional distress. The tabloid case collapsed when the editor
admitted he'd chosen her picture assuming she'd be dead by
now. The courts awarded Nellie $1.5 million in punitive and
compensatory damages.

**Hans Van Meergeren made himself a millionaire by
forging art masterpieces, but became so good at it that
he was almost executed for his work. Van Meergeren**

specialised in knocking off fake works by the great
Dutch artist Vermeer. He sold his first forgery in the
1930s for $250,000 and, during World War Two, created
and sold five more. One of these he sold to Hermann
Goering for $265,000. Van Meergeren thought he'd
pulled a fast one on the Nazis, but after the war the
Dutch Government had him arrested as a traitor: he
had sold a Dutch national treasure to the Germans.
The sentence was death by firing squad. Van
Meergeren protested that the painting had been a
fake, but no one believed him. The fake was that
perfect. Van Meergeren begged the court to let him
have a canvas and some paints in his jail cell and
proceeded to prove to them that he was capable of
creating fake masterpieces that could fool the entire
art world.

. When an ambassador for the Shah of Persia announced that he would be arriving in France, King Louis XIV of France made sure he received a fabulous royal welcome. The ambassador was put up in the Royal Palace and a huge ball and banquet was held in his honour. The King presented him with a portrait of himself framed in diamonds along with a vast array of other valuable gifts worth many millions of francs.

The ambassador was embarrassed at receiving these riches because the gifts from the Shah were still at sea and arriving in a few days. However, in the meantime, he presented the King with a small bag of jewels.

A few days later a message was delivered to the King that the ambassador would be presenting himself to the court – the treasures from the Shah had finally arrived. King Louis and Cardinal Richelieu waited. And waited. And waited. The ambassador never showed up and he and the priceless portrait were never seen again.

It turned out the so-called ambassador was an audacious con man. The 'jewels' he had presented to the King were just coloured glass.

In 1950s America, con men made an absolute fortune running a small ad in comic books and pulp magazines. The ad said simply: 'Learn something valuable for 50 cents'. Those who applied got a note back saying: 'Do not answer advertisements of this kind.'

. Italian vintners Giuseppe Massman and Benito Gatio made their fortunes selling supposedly 'fine wines' which were really made from rotten fruit they picked up off the ground at Rome's street markets. They didn't care what they put in it – mouldy dates, rancid figs, blackened bananas, pulped marrows and runner beans. It all went into the brew, along with neutral spirit to boost it. The strangest thing is that they sold literally millions of bottles over thirteen years and no one ever spotted the difference.

£ **When Jean-Claude 'Baby Doc' Duvalier, the 'President for Life' of Haiti, married his bride Michele in June 1980, the wedding cost an estimated $3 million, despite the fact that 90% of the island's population were on the point of starvation. During his fifteen years in power, the rancid little dictator managed to steal a badly needed $120 million from his wretched people, salting it away in numerous bank accounts as well as buying himself a $2.5 million apartment in Manhattan, a French chateau, three apartments in Paris and two more in New York, a $100,000 Ferrari, yacht and power boat.**

His wife Michele once went on a shopping spree to Paris and spent $2 million in a single visit. The Haitian Treasury picked up the tab. The pair were finally forced to flee in a coup in 1986, but still managed to fill an entire plane with furs, diamonds and national treasures as they departed ...

£. Although he was probably responsible for about 500 deaths, including those killed in the infamous 1929 'St Valentine's Day Massacre', Al Capone was never convicted on any charge relating to being a gangster.

The man they nicknamed 'Scarface' was too untouchable for that. He had the police and the courts in his pockets and virtually ruled Chicago. There was only one man tougher in the whole of America – the tax man.

In 1931 Al Capone was sentenced to eleven years for tax

evasion. By all accounts he was absolutely gobsmacked. 'I didn't know you had to pay tax on illegal earnings!' he protested as he was led away. Those illegal earnings amounted to many millions of dollars, almost all of it from bootlegging. In 1927 alone, Al Capone personally made $105 million. Although he was hardly pleased to be banged up, Capone was unrepentant about his business. 'When I sell liquor, it's bootlegging. When my patrons serve it on silver trays on Lake Shore Drive, it's hospitality,' he said.

He was released after eight years in jail but was already dying from syphilis. He still had enough money to afford experimental treatment, becoming the first man to have syphilis treated by antibiotics.

It didn't work. He died insane in January 1947.

In the 1980s, an inventive con artist took Wall Street to the cleaners to the tune of $200 million. At the age of just sixteen, Barry Minkow set up his own carpet-cleaning business in the garage of his parents' California home but he had no intention of ever cleaning a single carpet. Instead, he had set up his company, ZZZZ Best, solely to attract investors.

To raise the stake money for the company he staged burglaries for the insurance and borrowed $2,000 from his granny – then stole her pearls when she wasn't looking.

To help him run the fledgling company he employed a fanatical gun-toting Nazi who wore SS-style jewellery, and a giant albino who called himself 'the Ultimate White Man'. Together, they established another company, Interstate Appraisal Services, whose sole purpose was to give fake reports to potential investors showing how great it would be to invest in ZZZZ Best. It worked. By the time Barry was twenty-one, he had an estimated worth of $200 million and ZZZZ Best had still not cleaned a single carpet, ever. Barry became a hero to the Yuppies of Wall Street and Oprah Winfrey invited him on to her show, describing him as 'The Whiz Kid of Wall Street'.

It couldn't last though. To help him establish ZZZZ Best, Barry had ripped off early investors in a credit card scam. The *Wall Street Journal* got wind of this and began an investigation which exposed ZZZZ Best as an utter sham. Overnight, its stock market value collapsed. Barry was jailed for twenty-five years on fifty-seven counts of fraud, but only $62,000 of his assets were ever recovered. He had pulled off the most lucrative scam in Wall Street's history.

Chapter 6

I'M THE BOSS!

> *I believe the power to make money is a gift
> from God.*
> — *John D. Rockefeller*

It seems that for many people the accumulation of a huge fortune makes them think they are above the law. The sad reality is that in many cases this is absolutely true!

For example, Henry Flagler – John D. Rockefeller's business partner and a Florida real-estate developer – had his first wife committed to an asylum then tried to have their marriage dissolved. But, to his horror, he discovered that under Florida law insanity is insufficient grounds for divorce. However, ever grateful for his investment and previous charitable donations, the Florida legislature quickly revoked this inconvenient law for the powerful man, enabling Flagler to end his

marriage legally. The act became known as 'Flagler's Law'.

. To avoid paying tax, American Kenneth Dart, the billionaire plastic-cup manufacturer, renounced his US citizenship and instead became a citizen of Belize in Central America. He then got back into the US by getting himself appointed special Belizian diplomatic envoy to Florida.

Max Aitken, Lord Beaverbrook, the famous British press baron, attracted some sharp criticism for his business practices. H. G. Wells said of him, 'If Max gets to Heaven he won't last long. He will be chucked out for trying to pull off a merger between Heaven and Hell – after having secured a controlling interest in key subsidiary companies in both places, of course.'

. Columbia Pictures sent a private jet to fly Demi Moore from her home in Idaho to New York to attend the premiere of *A Few Good Men*. She was horrified to discover that her luggage would not fit side by side in the luggage hold. There was room only if it was stacked up. So she insisted Columbia send a different, larger jet to get her and dismissed the first ... Perhaps that's why in Hollywood she's known as 'Gimme Moore'.

Robert Maxwell loathed smoking. Employees who dared smoke in his presence were liable to be sacked on the spot. One day, getting into a lift in one of his buildings, he found it occupied by a man smoking a cigarette. 'How much do you earn?' Maxwell roared. '£75 a week,' the man replied. Immediately, Maxwell fished out his wallet and slapped £300 – a month's

wages – into the man's hand. 'You're fired!' he bellowed.

The man calmly pocketed the money and got out of the lift. Only later did Maxwell discover that the man was a courier just visiting the building, and didn't work for him ...

If his bullying didn't work, Hollywood mogul Louis B. Mayer would try to get his own way by crying ...

Successful salesmen are said to be able to sell snow to Eskimos. Well, self-made American millionaire Timothy Dexter did the next best thing – he sold coals to Newcastle and warming pans to the West Indies.

Born into a very poor family in 1747, Dexter had very little schooling. At sixteen he became an apprentice in the leather-dressing business and at twenty-two he set off for the thriving harbour at Newburyport, about forty miles from Boston, with just a few dollars in his pocket. He soon established a successful business there and within two years was married.

During the War of Independence he had invested his profits in European currency, worthless at the time because there was no trade between the continents. When the war ended in 1783 this currency became worth a fortune! Dexter then bought two large ships to export goods to Europe and the West Indies. On one occasion he was tricked into buying a huge consignment of warming pans for the West Indies. Ingeniously, he sold these as ladles for the huge molasses industry there. But he was tricked again when he sent two boatloads of coal to England, unaware there was already a successful coal mining industry in Newcastle. But as luck would have it, by the time the coal arrived the country was in the grip of a coal strike and he made simply enormous profits.

Despite his huge wealth, the snobbish New Englanders refused to accept Dexter into their society. To impress them he bought himself a huge country estate in New Hampshire and a title to go with it. Now living a lavish lifestyle, he wanted to know what his friends and colleagues thought of him. The best way to do this, he felt, was to stage his own death. After his passing away was announced he hid in the house and was gratified to see 3,000 people turn up to pay their last respects. Most people were kind and generous but his much despised wife didn't even shed a tear, which infuriated him to the point of physical violence.

By the time he really died – in 1806 – the gardens of his Massachusetts mansion had been filled with life-size statues of the forty-five men and women he admired most in the world, including George Washington, Napoleon and the

Goddess Venus. At the centre, larger than life, he'd placed his own statue, inscribed: 'I am the greatest man in the East'.

£ When Barbra Streisand flew into Washington to attend Bill Clinton's inauguration as US President, she was miffed to hear that she had not been given the biggest suite of rooms at the hotel. 'Who has?' she demanded. When told the occupants were Hillary Clinton's parents, Streisand demanded that they be thrown out so that she could have the rooms instead. The hotel concierge offered to help her find another hotel.

During the 1890s William Randolph Hearst's *New York Journal* was involved in a vicious circulation war with *The World*, published by Joseph Pulitzer. Hearst's accountant warned him that the battle was costing him half a million dollars a year. Hearst pondered the statistic then declared, 'Well at that rate I can only last another thirty years.'

> **H. L. Hunt was an eccentric billionaire oil baron who believed he had a 'genius gene' which it was his solemn duty to spread as far and wide as possible. To do this, he set up three different households, installed a wife in each and had fifteen children by them.**

A staunch patriot, William Lever – the man who established Lever Brothers – thought that his 'Sunlight Soap' could make a real difference to Britain's chances of victory in the First World War. Adverts told mums and wives to include a block of soap in their next parcel to the front because 'while such quality exists, victory is assured'.

The most memorable advert featured a soldier in the trenches and was headed 'The CLEANEST fighter in the world – the British Tommy.' The copy read like this: 'The clean, chivalrous fighting instincts of our gallant soldiers reflect the

ideals of our business life. The same characteristics which stamp the British Tommy as the CLEANEST FIGHTER IN THE WORLD have won equal repute for British goods. SUNLIGHT SOAP is typically British. Tommy welcomes it in the trenches just as you welcome it at home.'

However, this didn't stop Lever selling Sunlight Soap to the Germans as well until the Government stopped him.

> According to his former aide, Noah Dietrich, billionaire
> Howard Hughes had three principles:
> 1. Anyone can be bought so find out the price.
> 2. Use other people's money.
> 3. Any trouble, fire the sonofabitch.

Harry Cohn, president of Columbia Pictures, was nicknamed 'The meanest man in Hollywood'. His detractors weren't just talking about his incredibly stinginess either – they were also referring to the vicious, sometimes even monstrous way he treated everyone around him. The man who had also been nicknamed 'White Fang' delighted in his own lack of tact and manners and loved to spy on his employees. And, if he didn't invent 'the casting couch', he certainly took exploitation to new and more blatant heights. Legend has it that he fired Marilyn Monroe from Columbia because she spurned his advances. Frank Sinatra said of him, 'He's the type you like better the more you see him less.'

However, he had an unerring sense for what sort of films the public wanted to see – and owed it all to his backside. If while watching a movie, his bottom started to itch, he knew that the film would be a flop. You just can't buy that sort of talented posterior at any price, and it kept Cohn as president of Columbia for life. When he died in 1958, everyone attended his funeral, prompting one wag to say: 'It only proves what they always say – give the public something they want to see and they'll turn up to see it!'

Ivar Kreuger was one of the world's richest men in the 1920s, basically because the Swedish businessman lied about the value of his companies and wrote totally bogus financial reports. With investors falling over themselves to buy into his companies and banks

desperate to lend him money, Kreuger coined it in, becoming so wealthy that he personally loaned money to over a dozen countries including France, Poland, Greece and Spain.

Any bankers who doubted him would soon discover how powerful he was. In the middle of a meeting a phone would ring. 'It's Benito Mussolini,' he would tell the banker, and then proceed to tell off Il Duce in no uncertain terms, threatening that if he didn't get Italy's finances sorted out the fat lump of blubber would be in a world of trouble. The bankers were always impressed. Of course, the whole thing was a fake performance staged for their benefit.

No one caught on to what Kreuger was doing, and it took the Wall Street Crash of 1929 to bring him down. Ruined, Kreuger committed suicide and King Gustav of Sweden personally ordered all Swedish flags flown at half mast to mourn his passing. Only then was it discovered how many thousands of people Kreuger had ripped off during his business career. Financial investigators discovered that he'd stolen over half a billion dollars from his own companies between 1917 and 1932, and had allowed himself 'pocket money' of $180,000 a week …

The late Rumanian dictator Nicolae Ceaucescu shared Howard Hughes's fear of germs. When obliged to perform a walkabout he had his secret police find some likely candidates from the general public, had them locked away and regularly washed and disinfected for weeks, so that on the big day these people could then step forward to shake the dictator's hand …

. H. Ross Perot, head of the multi-billion dollar Electronic Data Systems Corporation, had a coral reef dynamited at his sea-front home in Bermuda because it interrupted the flow of the waves and made his yacht's propeller slip in the water.

> **Favouritism? When James VI of Scotland became king of England, he rented out the whole of Canada to the Earl of Stirling for just a penny a year.**

. If billionaire property magnate Donald Trump didn't exist, someone would have invented him. The man who made his name by developing large parts of Manhattan didn't start with nothing. In fact he started working in a Brooklyn-Queens real-estate business founded by his father that was worth $40 million.

The secret to his success was perception; a belief that if people *believed* you were the greatest then you *were* the greatest. He expanded this philosophy in his best-selling book: Trump: The Art of the Deal. His employees were sent out to buy vast quantities of this book, which put it on the best-seller list. These sales convinced other book buyers that it really was a best-seller and that they too should buy it – and so on. (Note to editor: Now there's a good idea!)

Trump was a speculator with real vision, and bought large parts of New York during the 1974–75 recession. At the peak of his success, Trump had the largest yacht in the world and owned the prestigious Trump Plaza, Trump Palace, Trump Parc and Trump Castle. He personified the eighties when greed, self-promotion and arrogance were seen as traits to be admired. He was feted everywhere he went and almost achieved rock-star adoration. But he also had his fair share of critics. He demolished an Art-Deco building to make way for Trump

Tower on Fifth Avenue, which the *New York Times* proclaimed was an act of 'aesthetic vandalism'. The tenants of these luxury apartments were in turn described as 'coke dealers, mobsters or those who may have gotten a touch too friendly with mobsters'. There's no denying the Midas touch Trump wielded. He built the Central Park Wollman Skating Rink in four months in 1986 for $2.1 million after the municipal government had spent six years and over $12 million trying to get the same job done – although they refused to allow him to call it Trump Ice, Inc.

Not someone who was embarrassed by his wealth, Trump's transport fleet included the world's largest private yacht, the 100-room *Trump Princess* bought from arms dealer Adnan Khashoggi for $30 million. This featured 200 separate phone lines, a hospital with operating theatre, a bullet-proof sauna and a hairdressing salon. For air travel he had the best non-military helicopter in the world (a Puma costing $2 million) and a Boeing 727 (costing $8 million). He also bought three casinos in Atlantic City ($220 million) and the New York Plaza Hotel ($400 million).

In 1988 Trump was estimated to be worth $1.7 billion. Two years later it was a different story. His net worth then was a negative $295 million. His fall from grace was dramatic. The credit on which he'd financed most of his deals dried up and venture after venture went bust. A 1990 *Newsweek* article described him as 'a parody of twentieth century capitalism; not tragedy but farce'. People who had praised Trump a few years earlier were now gloating at his decline.

But don't feel bad for him. Trump's bankers restructured his finances and imposed strict controls on his spending, limiting him to an allowance of just $375,000 per month. Bless him.

💰 Queen Elizabeth I imposed a tax on people wearing beards, as did Peter the Great of Russia. Many noblemen left Russia in disgust, to live their lives in exile with their beards. In France during the reign of King Francis I anyone seen wearing a beard or moustache was immediately put to death.

Peter the Great was more merciful. When he stopped his beard tax and made them illegal instead, he decreed that anyone caught with one would have each individual bristle removed with pliers...

> **When he visited Palestine in 1887, Edmond de Rothschild enquired whether the Wailing Wall in Jerusalem was for sale.**

💰 A shabbily-dressed man went up to one of the tellers in the Bank of Washington in the town of Spokane in February 1989 and asked her to validate his sixty-cent parking ticket.

She refused, so the man then approached the manager – who also refused. At this point the man revealed that he was fifty-nine-year-old customer John Barrier, who happened to have $1 million on deposit.

To the manager's horror he immediately closed his account and transferred the money to the rival Seafirst Bank down the road.

'If you have $1 in a bank or $1 million,' Barrier said, 'I think they owe you the courtesy of stamping your parking ticket.'

Carmel in California used to have a law prohibiting ice cream parlours. When Clint Eastwood became mayor there he declared that the town wasn't big enough for the law and him – so the law went.

. When Duchess Isabella of Rutland lost a front tooth, she insisted that her maid have her front tooth surgically removed – and donate it to her mistress.

> William Waldorf Astor had his private secretary release the news of his death and then lay low – just because he wanted to read his own obituaries.

Catherine the Great of Russia (1729–96) was horrified when her personal hairdresser told her she had dandruff. To prevent the news getting out – and possibly sparking a revolution – Catherine had her hairdresser locked up in an iron cage for three years.

Her son, Czar Paul of Russia, was equally sensitive about his hair. Anyone who dared mention that he was going bald was immediately flogged to death.

Ferdinand II of Sicily (1810–59) was so vain that even his picture on his nation's postage stamps had to be perfect. He made franking over his royal countenance an act of high treason. Fearful for their very lives, the members of the postal service worked for years to develop a frank that would fit around the King's picture without blemishing it.

What do you do if you've made a fortune and then go bankrupt? Most businessmen start again, building up their empire slowly but surely. But Joshua Abraham Norton, a nineteenth-century English trader, couldn't be bothered to claw his way back to the top again. He took a short cut and simply declared himself Emperor of the United States instead.

Norton had settled in San Francisco in 1853 and soon built a huge fortune by trading in coal, tea, flour and beef. They called him 'the merchant with the Midas touch'. Then he gambled everything on the rice market – and lost.

The strain of bankruptcy flipped Norton over the edge. In September 1859 he strode into the offices of the *San Francisco Bulletin* and told the editor to publish his Imperial Proclamation which established him as Emperor Norton I of the United States. Surprisingly, the proclamation was published and Norton set about ruling the country.

Among his policies were abolishing the Democratic and Republican parties, as well as Congress. In future, all the power would be vested in him alone, he announced. But he was not so grand as to neglect lesser duties. These included personal inspections of bus timetables, construction sites and sewage systems, while astride his official Imperial Bicycle. During these inspections and on his regular walkabouts around San Francisco to meet 'his' public, Emperor Norton wore an army officer's blue uniform with gold epaulettes, a tall black hat with a green plume and a heavy sabre by his side. He was usually accompanied by two mongrel dogs, Bummer and Lazarus.

His eccentric behaviour made him a popular character among the locals, who bowed when he walked past on his way to or from his Imperial Palace – a cheap flophouse down on Commercial Street. He issued his own home-made twenty-five and fifty-cent bank notes, which were accepted by local traders, and shopkeepers in the Bay area were also willing to pay him the small twenty-five cents weekly tax which he imposed. Theatres offered him free admission and patrons would often stand when he took his seat in the auditorium. He ate free at the best restaurants. The Central Pacific Railroad even gave him a pass for life. Policemen saluted him in the street and he renamed the San Francisco Police Department 'Norton's Imperial Constabulary', and marched proudly at the head of their annual parade.

He took a keen interest in international politics. He fired Abraham Lincoln for incompetence and advised Queen Victoria to dump Albert and come and share his Imperial Bedchamber instead. He also declared himself Protector of Mexico – a post he resigned a few years later, moaning that the place was too crazy for him to look after.

Emperor Norton I died aged sixty–one in 1880 with the newspaper proclaiming: 'The King Is Dead!'. Flags were hung at half mast and the city paid for a grand funeral, the likes of which were usually reserved for real royalty. Over 30,000 of his loyal 'subjects' attended his funeral. His obituary wisely said: 'The Emperor Norton had shed no blood, robbed no one and despoiled no country – which is more than can be said for most fellows in his line.'

£ President Calvin Coolidge was renowned for being economical with small talk at the dinner table, to the point of almost ignoring his guests. At one dinner party, where he had remained almost silent throughout, a lady diner turned to him and said, 'Mr President, I made a wager before I came out that I would be able to get you to say more than two words to me this evening.'

The President looked thoughtfully at her for a moment then said, 'You lose.'

Chapter 7

MIS-FORTUNES

Success is just a matter of luck.
Ask any failure.
— Anonymous

As much as some people have been very lucky by being in just the right place at the right time to make their fortune, so have others been in the right place at the right time and have still managed – often by sheer stupidity – to make completely the wrong decision and miss the one great chance in a lifetime to become seriously rich.

... Like Dick Rowe, the legendary A&R man working for Decca Records in the sixties. He is now almost as famous as the Fab Four for being the man who turned down The Beatles after hearing their demo record. He reportedly told the band's manager Brian Epstein: 'I'm sorry, but groups with guitars are on their way out ...'

Dick by name, dick by nature!

. In February 1970 a new author submitted the manuscript of a thriller he had just written to the publishers W. H. Allen. They returned it eight weeks later with a rejection letter, saying it 'had no reader interest'. The same novel was also turned down by four other publishers. Eventually, Hutchinson agreed to publish it and to date, close on nine million copies of Frederick Forsyth's *Day of the Jackal* have seen sold.

Nathaniel Bentley's life was not so much 'rags to riches' as 'riches to rags'. He inherited a fortune when his father died in 1760 and enjoyed life in style while running a very successful hardware shop (he ran his business from a splendid house in Leadenhall Street in London's East End). In his finery he moved in the most fashionable circles and was even a guest at the coronation of King Louis XVI. Soon he became engaged and announced a grand pre-wedding dinner at home. It was while preparing for this that news was brought to him of his fiancée's sudden and tragic death.

Nothing would ever be the same again for Nathaniel Bentley. From that day on he devoted himself entirely to his business, putting an end to the endless balls and banquets he attended. Friends expected him to come through this period of mourning but, instead, Bentley went into terminal decline. He gave up washing and changed his clothes only when they fell apart. Now known locally as 'Dirty Dick', his premises became known as the 'Dirty Warehouse', with cobwebs, soot and grime covering the once beautiful white exterior.

Filth was just as evident within the hardware shop – a thick layer of dirt and dust covered everything. Strangely, rather than discouraging business, more people actually visited him, just so they could meet the shop's strange owner. Letting the rest of his once fine house decay, Bentley himself lived in just one room. Here he had a gas range and one frying pan, sleeping on the floor in just an old, dirty and matted coat.

He lived this way for thirty years, somehow eking out a living. Eventually his lease expired and he was forced to leave. His fortune now gone, he walked from town to town until he reached the Scottish border. He died broke in a town called Haddington in 1809.

While his wife finished dressing, wealthy Williams Collins Whitney decided to have a quick bet at the gambling tables in their hotel. While he was waiting he managed to lose $385,000 – and that was a lot of money in the 1890s.

When Marvin Mitchelson, a millionaire Hollywood divorce lawyer, dumped a girlfriend, she got her revenge by informing the Internal Revenue Service that he had filed false returns.

He was convicted of tax fraud, sentenced to thirty months in prison and ordered to pay $2 million in back tax. The day he was sentenced he told the judge: 'This is the second saddest day of my life. My mother's death was the first.'

William Stern had the dubious honour of being the world's largest bankrupt, owing £104,390,000. The former millionaire agreed to pay the sum of £6,000 a year to pay off his debts, meaning that some of his creditors would have rather a long time to wait – over 1,700 years to be precise.

Turkish wrestler Yousouf Ishmaelo was immensely wealthy but, because he didn't trust anyone to look after his money for him, he took it everywhere he went in the form of gold ingots, carried inside a pouch worn round his waist. In 1898 he toured America with great success before returning to Turkey.

Unfortunately the boat on which he was travelling, the *Burgoyne*, hit a reef and rapidly started to sink. All the passengers survived the wreck except Ishmaelo. The weight of the gold bullion around his waist prevented him from swimming to safety and he went down with the ship.

. John Warburton devoted much of his life – and a good part of his fortune – to collecting rare and antiquarian books. The pride of his collection was fifty-eight first-edition plays, including many of Shakespeare's original works. He came home one day to find that a maid, Betsy Baker, had mistaken them for waste paper and had either burned them all or used them as pie bottoms. Only three survived.

£ Richard Burton once gave Elizabeth Taylor a 69.42-carat diamond worth over a million dollars. She later sold it to pay for her new husband, politician John Warner's, campaign expenses. 'If only I'd known I could have sent him the money in the first place and cut out the middle man,' Burton remarked dryly.

£. US actress Clara Bow – the original 'It Girl' from the 1920s – had a clause written into her contract with Paramount that she would receive a $500,000 bonus if she remained free of scandal during the length of the agreement. Sadly, even the lure of half a million dollars wasn't nearly as strong as her libido and she pretty quickly forfeited the money.

Other Hollywood stars with odd clauses in their contracts included Buster Keaton, who was prevented from smiling on screen, Joan Crawford, who had to be in bed by a certain time and Maurice Chevalier, whose contract was rendered void if he should ever lose his trademark French accent.

£ **MGM studio boss Louis B. Mayer turned down the chance to put Walt Disney under contract – and lost the studios the chance to own the entire Disney empire. He was convinced that the sight of a giant mouse, i.e. Mickey, on the big screen, could do irreparable harm to pregnant ladies.**

To be fair, Britain's then leading film magazine *The Picture Show* was also quick to condemn Mickey Mouse. The editor wrote, 'I think it is always a pity when cinema cartoonists can animate pretty creatures but choose to give screen life to vermin. One thing is sure – the British picturegoer could never come to enjoy the capering of a rodent.'

In 1877, Alexander Graham Bell offered to sell exclusive rights to the telephone to Western Union for just $100,000. They turned him down.

In August 1981 a wealthy Nigerian, Kizitio Idehem, withdrew nearly £250,000 from his bank in cash, placed it in a black bag and took a mini cab to a business appointment. En route he stopped to pop into a shop and asked the driver to wait a few minutes.

The driver, Kevin Butler, an Irishman from Finsbury Park, drove off with the bag and has never been seen to this day.

. The story of James Swan is a classic tale of rags to riches ... to rags to riches and then to rags again. Arriving in America from Scotland at the age of eleven, Swan quickly became a stout and loyal American patriot. He took part in the Boston Tea Party and fought at the Battle of Bunker Hill. The revolution over, he used his wife's inheritance to further his business interests and quickly became incredibly rich. Equally quickly, he lost it all again and, pursued by creditors, sailed for France.

Once there, he never forgot his love of America and, having amassed a second fortune he used a considerable part of it to pay off America's national debt – the money the revolutionaries had borrowed from the French. Having made such a huge contribution to the future of America you'd have thought that his adopted land would have come to his assistance when he needed help. Wrong. Eight years later, as his business crumbled, German creditors had him flung into debtor's prison. He languished there for twenty years until he died – and America did nothing to help him.

£ The grandfather of film star Lana Turner owned a half share in a new company that had started bottling a fizzy drink. He thought the drink's name would affect its saleability and wanted to change it – without success. In frustration he sold his fifty per cent. It's a pity really because Coca-Cola really caught on ...

A few years later, though, Coca-Cola had the chance to buy its rival, the Pepsi-Cola company, for a bargain $1,000. They turned it down, missing the opportunity to take over what would become their arch rival.

A very wealthy French landowner by the name of Foscue died because of his miserliness. He'd acquired his fortune by extorting huge rents out of struggling eighteenth-century French farmers and kept his money in a secret vault under the floorboards of his chateau.

He liked to spend time with his money and one day, while he was fondling his francs, the heavy trap door slammed shut. It was so well concealed that worried searchers looking for him failed to find it. It was also so heavy that no sound could escape.

No one knew what had happened to Monsieur Foscue until a long time later when the new owner of his house discovered the secret vault while having building work done. On opening the trapdoor Foscue's skeleton was found sitting next to his money. In desperation he had eaten banknotes, his candle and some of the flesh from his own arms before eventually dying.

£ Heavyweight boxing champion Joe Louis relied on his manager to submit his tax returns, but when he retired unbeaten in 1949 he discovered that he owed $1.25 million. The only way he could ever hope to repay that was by coming out of retirement and boxing his way out of financial troubles.

In 1950 he fought ten times but didn't come anywhere near paying the bill. He even resorted to wrestling to try and earn extra money.

Public outcry at this degrading spectacle led to the Internal Revenue Service limiting the outstanding tax to a level that was practical for Louis to pay off – an amount, in reality, that didn't even cover the interest outstanding on his debt.

A few days before his wedding to his fiancée Helen Borton, Terry Milner bought her a block of lottery tickets as a gift. When she failed to show up at the altar, Terry raced around to her home and discovered a note. It said that one of the tickets he'd bought her had won her £3 million. Now she realised she didn't want to marry him after all and had booked herself a trip around the world instead …

The wealthy Dutch matinee idol Lou Tellegen starred in dozens of hit Hollywood silent movies of the 1920s including *Silent Wives* and *The Redeeming Sin*. However, with the advent of the talkies he became a penniless, forgotten man. In 1934 he took off all his clothes and sat himself down in a circle he'd created from dozens and dozens of his best reviews and press cuttings. Using the gold scissors that had once cut out these articles he stabbed himself through the heart several times, preferring suicide to a life without stardom and wealth.

Dale Miller of Florida went on a bender to end all benders when he discovered he had won $6.6 million on the Florida state lottery. Coming back in an inebriated state to say the least, he ended up having a furious row with his wife and storming out again to sleep it off in his car. When he returned at noon the next day, his wife apologised and said to help make things better she'd tidied up the house for him. Dale rushed inside the house to find the winning ticket was missing. It had been thrown out with the rubbish. Dale spent two weeks going through the local garbage dump – but never did find the ticket. Asked by a reporter what he'd spend the money on if he ever did locate it, Dale said gruffly, 'Clean clothes and a divorce.'

. Daniel K. Ludwig made his fortune by building the first of the petroleum supertankers in the 1950s. He then invested in mining, oil and property and by 1957 was estimated to be the fifth richest person in the world. He was always a visionary with an ability to think a generation ahead. He foresaw the explosion in world communications in the 1980s but unfortunately, hadn't foreseen the equivalent explosion in computers. Instead, he anticipated a huge world paper shortage – one that he could exploit by finding a considerable piece of land on which to grow timber.

He chose the Amazon basin in Brazil and planned to clear a few million acres of forest and replace them with fast-growing trees, suitable for paper production. In 1967, aged seventy, he bought four million acres of the Upper Amazon by the River Jari and set to work. He laid 2,600 miles of new roads and forty-five miles of railway tracks. He spent $270 million on a paper mill and shipped this from Japan to the Amazon, complete with its own power plant. 35,000 labourers were hired to service the whole operation.

Less than three years after his ambitious plan got under way, Ludwig's project was floundering. The newly-planted trees would not flourish in the Amazonian soil. Termites devoured supplies and the workforce was decimated by malaria. Scientists the world over condemned the scheme and its threat to the ecology of the region. Ludwig would not give up though and spent nearly $200,000 a day to make his scheme work.

By 1982, however, he finally admitted defeat. The project was taken over by a consortium of twenty-seven Brazilian companies who radically scaled it down. As for Ludwig, he returned to the United States to lick his wounds – and ponder about the $1 billion he had lost.

Paperwork delayed an Arizona couple's divorce by eleven days. In that time, the husband won $2.2 million on the state lottery. Because they were still legally married at that time, the judge ruled the wife was entitled to twenty-five per cent.

There really was a 'Man who broke the bank at Monte Carlo', as the famous song goes. His name was Charles Deville Wells, a cockney who 'broke' the bank over a dozen times in 1891, scooping more than a million francs at the roulette tables. He became legendary, thanks to the song written about him, and returned in style to the casinos of Monte Carlo on board his own 300-foot yacht complete with glamorous lady friend and the money of dozens of people who wanted him to gamble on their behalf. Unfortunately, his winning streak failed to return with him.

He quickly lost everything and had to wire his investors for more money. He lost that too and was soon reduced to selling coal from the yacht's engine room for stake money. Eventually, the French got fed up and deported him back to London, where it was discovered that he'd raised his original stake money by conning people into investing in bogus inventions he'd supposedly created. In truth, the only successful thing he'd ever invented was the musical skipping rope – an idea he'd sold for £50 – and he was sentenced to eight years penal servitude at the Old Bailey in March 1893.

The last Shah of Iran once lost three quarters of a million pounds on a poker game.

. Mrs Maureen Wilcox of Massachusetts thought she'd double her chances of winning a fortune by entering both the Massachusetts and Rhode Island state lotteries, with a different set of numbers for each. One week, her numbers came up in both lotteries. She would have won two jackpots – except for the fact that her Massachusetts numbers came up on the Rhode Island lottery and her Rhode Island numbers were the winning combination on the Massachusetts lottery …

Grigory Romanov was one of the wealthiest and most influential Russians under the old Soviet regime. As a senior member of the Politburo and Mayor of Moscow, he was able to use his influence to get hold of

virtually anything. So when his daughter got married in June 1980 he was able to call up the director of Leningrad's Heritage Museum and ask to borrow Catherine the Great's priceless and exquisite china dinner service for use at the wedding. Naturally, he got his way and the dinner service was delivered to the wedding reception.

Unhappily, later on in the evening, one of the guests accidentally dropped a priceless teacup. Then, the entire reception assumed that they were being asked to make a traditional Russian toast and hurled the rest of the crockery into the fireplace ...

. The Great California Gold Rush of 1849 started entirely by accident. Gold was found clogging up a water mill on the land of cattle rancher John Sutter. Already a wealthy man, Sutter found himself potentially rich beyond his wildest dreams – but then word got out of the find and gold fever was ignited throughout America.

Thousands upon thousands of would-be prospectors descended en masse onto Sutter's land. They smashed down his fences, ignored his pleas to go away and set up two vast shanty towns on his land. Later, these shanty towns would become Sacramento and San Francisco. Unable to dislodge them, Sutter went to court to prove that the land – and the gold – was rightfully his. In 1855, the court ruled in his favour, by which time $220 million worth of gold had been found, but that didn't help. The hordes of prospectors responded by burning down the courtroom before turning their anger on Sutter himself. They blew up his house with dynamite, smashed down what was left of his fences and shot his cattle. They also shot dead one of his sons and another drowned trying to escape the mob. Far from ending up the richest man in America, the man who discovered gold in California ended up half-crazy, destitute and penniless, dying in a cheap hotel room in Washington.

Brazilian Vincente Brito de Queiroz appeared in person on TV to collect his $5 million lottery winnings from the state lottery – and was immediately identified by police as an escaped fugitive wanted for questioning in connection with the death of his wife …

. In 1989, millionaire wine merchant William Sokolin invested $300,000 in a single bottle of Chateau Margaux which had once been owned by President Thomas Jefferson. Later that same year, he held an auction at Manhattan's elite Four Seasons restaurant where he offered the bottle to 300 of the world's leading wine collectors. The reserve was set at $519,000. Unfortunately, before the bidding actually started, Mr Sokolin accidentally dropped the bottle and smashed it …

At school, Jerry Lewis's classmates used to call him 'Id' – which was short for 'Idiot'. That's an equally appropriate nickname for the TV executives who, in 1963, signed Lewis up for a five-year contract worth $12.5 million to make a TV show. The public hated it and it was scrapped after just three weeks … Jerry was the only one laughing – all the way to the bank.

. In AD 193 the Roman Empire was officially sold off to the highest bidder. A Roman senator called Didius Julianus put in the highest bid of 300 million sesterces and was proclaimed emperor. He lasted sixty-six days before being murdered by a Roman general who then proclaimed himself emperor … for nothing.

The film star John Barrymore became an alcoholic at the age of fifteen. In a desperate attempt to dry him out, his family later took him out on a yacht for a long sea voyage. Despite their best efforts, Barrymore managed to stay drunk the whole time by secretly siphoning off alcohol from the boat's engine cooling system. He earned over $4 million in his lifetime, but drank and frittered it all away and died owing $75,000.

If you think you have tax problems spare a tear for American country singer Willie Nelson. In 1990 the Internal Revenue Service presented him with a bill for $32 million in back taxes, penalties and interest. Nelson blamed his accountants, claiming that their bad advice caused previous underpayments. After long negotiations the IRS agreed to reduce the liability to 'only' $9 million, payable in three years.

Nelson paid his tax bill after auctioning property, handing over the damages from his court case against his accountants, accepting donations from loyal fans and selling the rights to a new album called *Who'll Buy My Memories: The IRS Tapes*.

After the last payment was made Nelson's lawyer said, 'Willie is happy to be done with it. He has a very good relationship with the IRS now.'

Huntington Hartford inherited $100 million in 1958 but squandered it on various ill-advised projects. He spent half a million dollars trying to establish an artists' colony in California (no one was interested), $7 million on an art museum in Manhattan (it soon closed), $8 million on starting and running a magazine (no one bought it), $30 million on buying an island in the Bahamas and building a golf course (which proved unpopular).

£. Child star Jackie Coogan, the bright-eyed loveable little scamp who acted alongside Charlie Chaplin in *The Kid*, earned $4 million before he was twenty-one – but saw very little of the money. The money was held in trust for him until his twenty-first birthday but, just before the big day, his father was killed in a car crash. His mother quickly remarried and the pair refused to hand over Jackie's money. He fought them for four years during which time, knowing they were going to lose eventually, the couple delighted in spending as much of poor Jackie's money as was physically possible, morning, noon and night. By the time the courts stopped them, Jackie's $4 million fortune had been frittered away to just $126,000.

Jackie's misfortune didn't end there though. His cute looks deserted him as he grew up and he ended up playing 'Uncle Fester' in 'The Addams Family'!

£ Scott Wenner of Texas won $10 million on the state lottery – and then was told that his winning ticket was forfeit because the shop he'd bought it from was unlicensed ...

Susan Evans sent her boyfriend out to get her national lottery ticket. Unfortunately, he got stuck in a queue and the lottery closed just as the ticket was being processed, rendering it invalid. That night, all six numbers came up. One second earlier, and Sue would have won an £8.5 million jackpot ...

£. It was H. Gordon Selfridge who had the idea of bringing the American-style department store to Britain – and it was an immediate success for the forty-five-year-old American nicknamed 'Handsome Harry'. When Selfridge's first opened in 1909, it took over sixty police officers to control the crowd of shoppers. Advertising itself as 'The World's Most Beautiful Store', Selfridge's claimed to have issued 600,000 exclusive invitations for its grand opening – 'but if you haven't received one, come along anyway', it said.

A workaholic for most of his life, H. Gordon was interested in the minutest details of business, from the sharpness of his employees' pencils to the state of their oral hygiene. However, when his wife died in 1918 he became a changed man and his usually impeccable business sense went to pot. While out nightclubbing at London's sleazy Kit-Kat Club, he met a pair of identical twins who danced under the stage name 'The Dolly Sisters'. From then on they were his first love, not business. They had carte blanche to walk into Selfridge's and help themselves to whatever they wanted – free of charge. And they did. Day after day after day. When they weren't shopping, they could be found on the arms of H. Gordon himself at Europe's finest casinos, gambling away vast chunks of his hard-earned money. When they – or their precious lap dog – got hungry, H. Gordon would charter an aeroplane to fly in their favourite ice cream or dog food. One of the gifts he presented to Jenny Dolly was a four-carat diamond set in the shell of a live tortoise. In ten years, H. Gordon spent over £8 million on the sisters … but of course it couldn't last.

Alarmed by H. Gordon's incessant spending and the Dolly Sisters' frequent raids on their most expensive merchandise, the board of Selfridge's edged him out and the sisters quickly dumped him. Selfridge was given a pension of just $8,000 a year – out of which he was supposed to pay back the $2 million he owed to the store.

Selfridge eventually died poor and alone in his small flat in Putney, still owing £1,650,000 to the tax man and considerably more to the store that still bears his name.

In 1886 a gold prospector named Sors Hariezon sold a claim he had made on a farm in Witwatersrand in the Transvaal. He was glad to take £10 for it and moved on. For the next ninety years, gold mines on or near his claim produced over a million kilos of gold a year – over seventy per cent of the Western world's gold supply. Hariezon's bad luck didn't end there … he was eaten by a lion shortly afterwards!

The first oil to be discovered in America was found by farmers in Pennsylvania. Some sold it as a medicinal cure for gout and fallen arches. Less enterprising farmers, dismayed that their water supply contained 'black glue', sold off their land for a pittance and moved away …

Chapter 8

MORE MONEY THAN SENSE

> *If God came into my room, I'd obviously be awed, but I don't think I'd feel humble. I might cry – but I know He'd dig me like mad...*
> – Marc Bolan

Some people have a lot of common sense, but never make any real money. For others, making a lot of money seems to make them a little unhinged. Perhaps the two somehow go hand in hand – it's their very eccentricity that makes them the kind of unique individual who is able to go on to win fame and fortune. Whichever way you look at it, some people have a lot more money than sense.

An obvious twentieth-century example is Michael Jackson. Has he got more money than sense? Well, make up your own mind ...

Bubbles, his pet chimp, had twenty designer outfits and his own hotel room whenever he travelled with Michael on tour.

One day, Jackson entertained himself by sitting on the floor of his living room, tearing up $100 bills and throwing them up in the air saying, 'Isn't it pretty? Money makes the best confetti.'

At one stage, Jackson visited Disneyland up to four times a day, wearing an assortment of wigs, fake beards, hats, glasses and false noses to disguise himself. In the end he abandoned this idea and wore a big coat, travelling around the theme park in a wheelchair just so he could get pushed right to the front of every queue.

In Michael Jackson's Neverland Ranch in Southern California there's a Treasure Room that contains a glass case containing $1 million in jewels, porcelain figures of him alongside Disney characters and a $200,000 portrait of him, Albert Einstein, Abraham Lincoln, George Washington, the Mona Lisa and ET, all wearing sunglasses and a white sequined glove.

. Born in 1792, wealthy English landowner Sir Thomas Phillipps was obsessed with owning a copy of every book in the entire world – and almost succeeded. By the time he died he owned more than 100,000 books and at least 60,000 manuscripts – a collection larger than that held by all the university libraries in Cambridge.

The books were kept at his country house, Middle Hill,

mostly in crates or in heaps on the floor. He acquired books quicker than he could unpack and catalogue them. In 1863 the collection outgrew the house and with the aid of 160 men and 103 wagons drawn by 230 horses, he moved to Thirlstaine House near Cheltenham. Here he decided to shelve his books properly and rode from room to room on horseback, supervising the installation of shelves.

He died in 1872 but so vast was his collection, that parts of it were still being auctioned off or sold a century after his death.

Born into a wealthy eighteenth-century Swiss banking family, Carl Stommfelder never had to do a real day's work in his life – which probably explains why he weighed over 290lbs at the age of twenty-five. His mind started to go after he fell into a cesspool while trying to evict a farmer. His weight made rescue impossible and he was forced to wallow in the stinking muck until someone could find a rope and tackle. After that, he regularly had six or seven baths a day to try and clean off the smell that haunted him.

As he grew keener on bathing, he had a giant bath full of inflated pillows made from sheep's stomachs made for him. One day in 1760, he climbed into the bath and refused to ever come out again. He ate, slept and even had sex with his housekeeper in the tub. In total, Carl spent forty-three years in the bathtub until the day he died in 1803. His last request was to be buried in his beloved tub, but the request was ignored on the grounds that he was a loony.

It seems a reasonable conclusion.

Victoria Woodhull first met Cornelius Vanderbilt when she offered to cure the ailing millionaire with her special healing powers. She also offered him stock market tips courtesy of her spirit guide – a long-dead Greek philosopher named

Demosthenes. While Demosthenes may have known something about the nature of existence, he proved to know bugger all about stocks and shares and lost Vanderbilt a lot of money. Gently, he suggested to Victoria that he knew more about business than her spirit guide and ended up giving her share tips which made her a very wealthy woman indeed.

Armed with Vanderbilt's priceless knowledge, Victoria and her sister opened the very first brokerage office to be run by women on Wall Street in 1870. They would have done exceptionally well – except that Victoria couldn't keep her mouth shut about her rather unusual beliefs. Almost immediately, Victoria put herself forward as a candidate for President of the United States and, in her political rallies, started advocating such unusual policies as free love, legalised prostitution, magnetic faith healing, easy divorce and vegetarianism. The 'free love' bit intrigued the voters in particular – and they wanted to know whether she practised it as well as preached it. She told the truth in a pamphlet – and spent the next six months behind bars for distributing an obscene publication. Later, she was to flee America, settle down with a respectable old banker and deny to her dying day that she had ever done anything improper …

> **The Russian Grand Duke Constantine liked to while away the hours shooting live rats out of a cannon.**

For reasons best known to himself, Sir Frank Crisp, a leading solicitor in the late 1800s, decided that what his estate at Friar Park in Oxfordshire was lacking was a 100–foot high scale replica of the Matterhorn. In 1896, he told his gardeners to put that right immediately and set them about constructing the mini–mountain from 20,000 tonnes of millstone grit and topping it off with an authentic piece of the summit of the Matterhorn. Unfortunately for the gardeners, Crisp wasn't one hundred per cent convinced about the accuracy of the finished model and ordered them to demolish it and start all over again.

They did.

No, still not right. Start again.

The wretched gardeners had to complete the task several times over before Crisp was finally satisfied. The mountain now complete, Crisp then set about building a massive and elaborate grotto underneath it, including a vast subterranean hall which is home to hundreds of garden gnomes.

Over the years, the weird construction fell into disrepair, and it was left to former Beatle George Harrison to restore it to its true glory when he purchased the estate in 1969.

. Thomas Gibson Bowles, the wealthy owner of *The Lady* magazine, was a famed Victorian eccentric. He made his two poor long-suffering daughters wear nothing but sailor suits until they were seventeen years old and then on their seventeenth birthdays permitted them to buy one gown each – provided it was in the style worn by Marie Antoinette over 150 years before! He also drove them mad by making impulsive, spur-of-the-moment decisions – like to emigrate to China. On one occasion, his loyal daughter Dorothy had to get the entire household contents packed, settle finances, dismiss the staff and arrange transport to China – in just three days. She had just completed the task when her father stuck his hand out of the door, frowned and said, 'My dear child, it's raining. We won't go.' Amazingly, he was not murdered on the spot …

Thomas – or Cap'n Tommy as he was known – was also addicted to steam baths, and insisted on taking with him wherever he went a mobile steam bath of his own rather unique design. It consisted of a number of dog kennels, arranged in a line some fifty yards long. The Cap'n would climb into the first kennel, which was lined with bricks and served as the actual steam room. Then, after spending about fifteen minutes in there, he would emerge stark naked and run up and down the row of kennels while his footmen stood on top of them and hurled buckets of ice cold water over him.

Elvis Presley once owned a pet chimpanzee called Scatter. The chimp wore tailor–made suits and liked to get drunk and smash up Elvis's telephones.

Benjamin Disraeli had all four legs of his bed positioned in bowls full of salty water to ward off evil spirits. If you think that's strange, for thirty-three years his wife saved all his hair trimmings and squirrelled them away in bags.

Franklin D. Roosevelt, the thirty-second president of the United States, was a great practical joker. He often attended functions at which he was introduced to hundreds of strangers. He soon realised that most people he exchanged pleasantries with paid little attention to what he actually said. Putting this to the test at a White House party, he muttered to every person he shook hands with, 'I murdered my grandmother this evening.'

Only one person that evening responded to his confession: an eminent Wall Street banker who said, matter-of-factly, 'Well, I'm sure she had it coming.'

During his bouts of madness King George III was, thankfully, imaginative rather than cruel. Unlike many monarchs whose mental illness took the form of savage sadism, George blissfully resided in a bizarre and gentle la-la land. Among his many delusions, he was convinced that London was under the sea and that one of the Queen's ladies-in-waiting was really his wife. When his real wife tried to free him of the illusion, he accused her of being mad and needing to be locked up. He planted 4lbs of beefsteaks in the royal gardens hoping to grow beef trees and believed he'd given birth to a pillowcase, whom he named Prince Octavius. To celebrate the birth of the pillowcase, he duly knighted a number of his servants and page boys.

He thought the queen of hearts from a pack of playing cards had sent him a bunch of grapes, knighted one of his doctors by emptying a chamber pot over his head and believed that he, his doctor and a lady-in-waiting were really the Holy Trinity. During one bout of madness, he even insisted on ending every single sentence he uttered with the word 'peacock'. For reasons now sadly lost to us, his nickname was 'Old Nob'.

£ Ernest Onians was the millionaire manufacturer of Tottenham puddings. When he died in 1985, his executors found they were unable to get into his Georgian mansion because it was literally piled floor to ceiling with priceless antiques. In the last forty years of his life he had spent millions of pounds on furniture, paintings, clocks, sculptures and musical instruments – but didn't have the time or inclination to look after them. Outhouses and sheds on his estate were similarly packed with valuable objects.

Despite his wealth, Onians always wore the scruffiest clothes. As the house filled with antiques his servants had to leave. There was simply less and less room for them. Burglars once broke in but only took a small amount of cash. They totally ignored the vast horde of antiques, mistaking them for a junk pile.

. Film actor James Stewart had a second career that has remained virtually unknown to this day. He was a yeti smuggler. His wealth allowed him to indulge in his passion to discover the truth about the Abominable Snowman, and he secretly sponsored a number of expeditions to the Himalayas. In 1959, parts of an alleged Yeti's hand were discovered and smuggled out of Tibet for analysis. Stewart personally hid the hand in his suitcase and smuggled it into London for tests …

> **King Henry VIII liked roast beef so much he officially knighted it. That's where the term 'Sirloin' comes from …**

George 'Beau' Brummell must have inherited his dress sense from his grandfather, a valet. However his fortune came from his father, private secretary to Lord North, the Prime Minister, and who rather astutely married an extremely wealthy heiress.

Brummell's wealth enabled him to become accepted in London society and he became good friends with the Prince of Wales. The Prince awarded him a commission in the exclusive 10th Light Dragoons and his smart hussar's uniform began his lifelong obsession with clothes and looking good.

Brummell soon bought himself out of the army, not wishing to get involved in any real soldiering in case he – or worse still – his uniform, got dirty. Free to mingle with the cream of society once more, he devoted all his time to his appearance, becoming the original – albeit a little eccentric – dandy and the epitome of style.

His clothes were simple yet elegant but it was his attention to detail that gave him his reputation. Brummell was such a perfectionist it took him three hours to tie his cravat. The slightest crease in the wrong place and he would fling the cravat off, demand a new one and begin all over again. He changed his shirts three times a day and sent them to the country to be laundered just so they came back smelling of new-mown hay. It took three people to make his gloves; one specialising in just the thumbs! To make sure his shoes and boots had the best possible shine, his valet would rub them with the froth of champagne – including the soles.

But to make sure his shoes remained clean he insisted that his sedan chair was actually brought inside his house in Chesterfield Street. This way he would avoid the risk of getting them dirty on the pavement. Other extremes he went to included not raising his hat to a lady, in case he could not replace it at exactly the right angle, and not turning his head to talk to someone at a dinner table – in case he creased his cravat.

For many years Brummell was the toast of society until one day while out walking in London he chanced upon an acquaintance and the Prince of Wales. Jokingly, Brummell gestured at the Prince of Wales and said to his acquaintance, 'Who's your fat friend?' The Prince of Wales was not amused and Brummell's popularity in polite society plummeted.

He continued to spend his inheritance on his clothes and gambling until he was penniless. Unable to keep up with fashion, he went insane and died alone in an unfashionable French asylum in 1840 aged sixty-two.

What would you do if you had £60 million? Buying yourself a week on board the decrepit Russian Mir space station would probably never occur to you, but then you're not Peter Llewellyn, a British tycoon with a passionate desire to go into space.

In April 1999, Llewellyn pledged £60 million to RKK Energia, the state-controlled company that runs the space station, to pay for his bed and board. The Russians are rubbing their hands with glee because Mr Llewellyn's money alone will cover half of Mir's annual maintenance fees. However, before they'll let him loose in their space station, the Russians are still insisting that he will have to undergo weeks of cosmonaut training at Star City, the HQ of the Russian Space Agency.

Eccentric French millionaire Henri Blanchard liked to boast he had nerves of steel. To prove it, on 9 May 1903, he climbed alone into a circus cage with eight lions and fired a pistol at a target, hitting centre each time. The lions were too puzzled by his absurd behaviour to eat him!

In 1986, a woman named Judith Richardson Haimes was awarded over $1 million in compensation – for loss of her psychic powers! She claimed that a brain scan performed on her by doctors looking for a tumour had robbed her of her ability to see the future, which had earned her $50,000 a year reading people's auras and helping the police to solve crimes. Her son had also been killed in a car crash and – she claimed – if she'd had her powers she'd have been able to warn him. The award was later overturned on appeal.

Sir Francis Galton, the wealthy cousin of Charles Darwin, was an eminent scientist and the founder of intelligence testing. He is perhaps less well known for devising a beauty map of Britain, recording the density of beautiful women in each major town or city. He did this by travelling up and down the country with a pocket counting device of his own invention. Every time he met a pretty girl he recorded it. After months of research he concluded that London has the highest proportion of beautiful women – and Aberdeen the lowest.

Sir Francis did a lot of thinking and in order that his brain didn't overheat, invented a hat which featured tiny shutters that could open or close, allowing cool air to circulate around his head.

Canned food millionaire H. J. Heinz kept an 800lb, fifteen–foot long alligator in a glass tank on the roof of his factory in Pittsburgh. He thought his employees might enjoy seeing it. It probably also deterred them from asking for a pay rise.

Wealthy Sir Vauncey Harper–Crewe inherited the huge Calke Abbey in Derbyshire from his father, Sir John, in the 1880s. He rarely left the mansion and communicated with his daughters by writing to them. Nothing wrong in that, you might think – except they all lived in the same house.

Sir Vauncey was an avid collector of, well, anything really. He bought stuffed birds and animals, paintings, furniture, prints, swords, butterflies, shells, books – you name it and he hoarded it. When he filled one of the rooms at Calke Abbey with specimens he simply locked the door for good, and began to fill the next room.

Sir Humphrey Davy, the wealthy inventor of the coalminers' Davy Lamp, was a keen fisherman and used to dress all in green in order to take on the appearance of a bush at the water's edge. One of his

contemporaries commented, 'Davy flattered himself that he resembled vegetable life as closely as it was possible to do.'

He abandoned any pretence at camouflage when it came to shooting, being concerned about the accuracy of his fellow hunters. To make sure he wasn't shot by mistake he always wore brightly coloured clothes, and in particular a red wide-brimmed hat.

. Walt Disney used to relax by playing with a train set. In his case however the train was large enough for him to ride on. The track circled his estate for half a mile, including a tunnel beneath his flower beds. But out of keeping with his wholesome image was his bizarre fondness for staging dramatic train crashes so that he could survey the destruction. Once, after buying two new engines, he told George Murphy (then an actor but later a US senator), 'Boy, we're sure going to have some wrecks now!'

The scientist Henry Cavendish inherited a vast fortune from his father – and was a millionaire even by contemporary standards. His particular eccentricity was his shyness. Although he was a brilliant scientist and a distinguished member of the Royal Society he found it difficult to talk to people. This shyness actually cost him the recognition of an important discovery – Ohm's Law. Ohm made the same discovery much later but wasn't as reluctant to tell anyone about it.

Cavendish was so shy that he didn't like talking to his servants. He communicated instead with them by leaving notes around the house. He once met one of his maids on the staircase and was so shaken by the experience that he had a separate staircase built for his exclusive use – to prevent the same thing ever happening again.

To reduce the number of occasions on which he had to leave his home, he had one of the rooms converted into a vast laboratory and one of the bedrooms converted into an observatory.

When he did have to leave the house, to attend meetings of the Royal Society for example, he prevented people from striking up a conversation with him by talking continually to himself in a high-pitched voice. He never spoke about 'trivial matters' like his wealth and when he died in 1819 he left his cousin George over £1,175,000 – money he'd been completely disinterested in.

Phileas Fogg, the millionaire hero of Jules Verne's *Around the World in Eighty Days* was based on the adventures of real American millionaire George Train, who was also known as 'The Great American Crank'.

In July 1870, Train – who ironically had made his fortune founding the Union Pacific Railroad – set out to travel around the world, not because of a wager but because he was simply bored. The journey took him precisely eighty days – including the thirteen days he spent in a French jail when mistaken for an anarchist revolutionary. He was forty-one when he made the journey – and did it twice more during his lifetime, cutting the time for a complete circumnavigation to just sixty days. A genuine character, he managed to get thrown in jail fifteen times in his life and was often followed by the spies of at least five different nations, who didn't know what he was up to but thought he must be up to something …

Like so many millionaires, as he grew older he grew stranger. He constantly ate peanuts, believing they would allow him to live to the age of 150 and, instead of shaking hands when meeting other people he would firmly shake his own hand instead. He refused to talk, and communicated via a writing pad to prevent his 'psychic energies' from being dispersed, and wrote hate–filled articles about the evils of mail order companies ...

£ **When Jack Mytton inherited his huge fortune in the early 1800s he was determined to enjoy himself, even if this meant behaving in a reckless manner, endangering his health, the health of his friends and anyone unfortunate enough to be around him.**

Mytton was born in Halston, near Shrewsbury, in 1796 and lived a wild childhood. Expelled from Harrow School, he had a short career in the army before being deemed unsuitable for any sort of discipline whatsoever. He lived for hunting and shooting – and nearly died for it too, dashing about the countryside on Baronet, his one-eyed charger. No jump was too high. No brook was too wide. And no waters were too icy for wading in. His riding exploits became legendary. He was the Evel Knievel of his time. On one occasion he jumped his horse off a hotel's second-storey balcony on to the street (how the horse got on to the balcony in the first place is anybody's guess). Another time he tried to warm his horse up by letting it drink an entire bottle of port. Once he bought a female brown bear on impulse and kept it at the family home. He even rode it in to dinner, scattering frightened guests in every direction and throwing handfuls of banknotes at anyone brave enough to catch them. Quite naturally, it bit him a few moments later when he dug his spurs in.

He also tried to leap over a field gate with his horse and carriage, completely wrecking it in the process, and deliberately tipped his carriage over on

another occasion just because his companion said he
had never been in an accident. Another time he
waited until his guests had left after dinner, changed
his clothes, grabbed a mask and two pistols, then rode
across country to intercept their carriage. As he
approached them Mytton shouted, 'Stand and
deliver', and fired his guns. His guests turned and
fled, with Mytton chasing after them for several miles,
firing wildly. This was his idea of a great lark. It's no
wonder he soon got the nickname 'Mad Jack'.

Fancying himself a bit of a medical man, the

Squire devoted a considerable time to trying to devise
a cure for hiccups. In the end, he claimed to have
found the perfect cure – but it involved putting on a
night shirt and then setting fire to it, so it never
caught on.

His extravagances were legendary. He owned 150

pairs of riding breeches, 700 pairs of boots, 1,000 hats and 3,000 shirts. But, despite this wardrobe, he sometimes preferred to be stark naked, especially when he was outdoors in the dead of winter, chasing ducks around the marshland. By 1831 the cost of running his kennels and stables (not to mention his drinking habits) had plunged him heavily into debt and he fled to France to escape his creditors. He returned voluntarily to face the music in 1834, only to be jailed in a debtors' prison, where he died aged just thirty-seven.

His funeral, like the man himself, was larger than life and thousands of spectators lined the route, shedding a tear for their local squire who'd given them so much to talk about.

Sophisticates may have hated him, but the poor folk definitely liked him, not least because he absent-mindedly dropped money wherever he went, and for entertaining them by staging boxing matches between himself and wild dogs and bears.

. Doris Duke was the original 'poor little rich girl'. Her father, James Duke, had founded the American Tobacco Company and Doris inherited $300 million when she was just thirteen.

She led an exotic life, divorced twice and enjoyed a stream of lovers who included Errol Flynn and General George S. Patton. One of her favourite hobbies was belly-dancing and her two pet camels had the run of her Beverley Hills mansion (she gave a coming-out party for both of them). She could also be as mean as she was extravagant, thinking nothing of paying $3,000 for a single bottle of wine, but deducting money from her servants' wages if they broke or even damaged a glass.

She had few friends in the world but was quite close to

Imelda Marcos, her neighbour on Honolulu. It was Duke who posted $5 million in bail for Marcos when she was indicted on fraud and embezzlement charges. To the surprise of her family she legally adopted a thirty-five-year-old former belly dancer Chandi Heffner, who she believed was the reincarnation of her daughter who had died shortly after being born in 1940. Her gifts to Chandi included a $1.5 million ranch in Hawaii and a $5 million legacy in her will.

'Moon the Loon' they called him, and The Who's eccentric drummer did his best to live up to his wild and crazy reputation. No hotel room was safe when Keith was in town. During his life he paid out no less than £200,000 in damages to hotels around the world for his little escapades, like taking an axe to hotel furniture on a whim.

In an interview, Pete Townshend recalled how Keith once bought 500 powerful Cherry bombs and kept blowing up the toilets in their hotels. 'We were thrown out of every hotel we stayed in,' he recalled. 'The Holiday Inns were phoning round saying, "Don't let this group stay, because they'll blow the place up", and it got to the point where they were asking for $5,000 deposit to let us stay in even the shoddiest hotels.' Townshend recalled his nerves finally went when Keith blew up the hotel manager's wife's room in an explosion that rocked the whole hotel.

'The momentum is still there when I come off stage. I'm like an express train or an ocean liner. It takes me two or three miles to stop,' Keith explained – but he was no better behaved between tours. His house in Malibu was next door to Steve McQueen. He drove the film star mental by blatantly spying on McQueen's wife Ali McGraw through a telescope and riding his motorbike back and forth over McQueen's beautiful lawns.

He was thrown off a British Airways jet in the Seychelles

when he stormed the cockpit and tried to play his drumsticks on the control panel, and caused outrage by wandering the streets of London dressed as a Nazi storm trooper – or a nun.

To many, it seemed like Moon had a death wish. He once drove a new Lincoln Continental into a hotel swimming pool and blew himself up live on American television. Moon had a technician rig his drums to explode during the finale of their set. The two got drunk, used way too much gunpowder and Moon was blown backwards through the scenery by the sheer force of the blast, while Pete Townshend's hair caught fire. Undeterred, Moon staggered back to take a bow, covered in blood and with his arms peppered with pieces of shattered cymbal.

If he had a death wish, he finally got his own way when he succumbed to a drugs overdose. It was how he would have wanted it. He once said his greatest fear was 'having to grow up'.

Gordon Bennett! There really was a Gordon Bennett – James Gordon Bennett to be precise, the proprietor of the *New York Herald* newspaper in the late nineteenth century. No one has really been able to work him out. On the one hand, he was a philanthropist, setting up soup kitchens for New York's poor and personally giving $100,000 for an Irish relief charity and paying for Stanley to go in search of the missing Dr Livingstone. And on the other, he was a bit of a nutter. He lost his fiancée and his place in high society after publicly urinating into her fireplace in the middle of her New Year's Party and being ejected from her home by the scruff of the neck. His favourite pastime was to run into a restaurant, yank the tablecloths off the tables, sending hot food and drinks cascading all over the alarmed diners, then stuff a wad of notes into the manager's hand before running out again.

He once arrived at a Parisian restaurant and, finding that all the tables were occupied, bought the restaurant on the spot for one million francs from its bewildered proprietor. His first act as owner was to have the waiters throw all the diners out into the street and then to settle down in the middle of a now empty restaurant and tuck into his favourite meal of mutton chops. After the meal, he gave the head waiter the deeds to the restaurant and told him he could keep it, provided he always reserve a table for Gordon Bennett and always kept mutton chops on the menu.

Incidentally, the waiter, who was named Ciro, went on to become an internationally acclaimed restaurateur in his own right.

Adolphus Cooke, a wealthy Irish landowner, believed that all animals were actually reincarnated people. One particular turkey on his estate, for example, was his dad and he insisted that all his servants and estate workers doff their caps to it and wish it a good day. Shortly before his death, he insisted his workers dig luxury foxholes all over the estate, as he was convinced he'd come back as a fox ...

'Mad, bad and dangerous to know' George Gordon, the sixth Lord – better known as the poet Byron – used his family's wealth to finance his writing career, and a life of debauchery and decadence. On hearing that no pet dogs were allowed in his college rooms at Cambridge, he bought himself a bear. In between sleeping with several of his college chums, having an affair with his own sister and carrying on with Lady Caroline Lamb, he apparently used to pounce on hapless chambermaids 'like a thunderbolt'. To keep his good looks and to try to tame his naturally rather obese figure, he often put his hair in rollers and was addicted to laxatives.

The Comtesse de Noailles was one of the world's truly great hypochondriacs, her bizarre fears matched only by her bizarre remedies. She was terrified if the wind blew in an easterly direction and would never leave the house when it did. While out travelling, she constantly checked the wind direction and if easterly winds developed she would demand the train be halted immediately so she could get home. An early pioneer of 'alternative medicine', her favoured cure-all was cow flatulence. No, seriously, it was. She always kept a herd of cows tethered under her open bedroom window at night so that their 'vapours' would waft up and make her healthy as she slept.

Another favourite was to sleep with her head wrapped in socks filled with squirrel fur and to stretch the skin of a Norwegian wild cat across her chest. Whether any wild cat would do, or if it particularly had to be Norwegian to work, I don't know.

Now, we may laugh, but the Comtesse lived to the ripe old age of eighty-four, so maybe she knew something we don't …

Unfortunately for her daughter Maria, she also insisted on inflicting her views on her, even when she was away at school. She arranged for her own cow to be tethered in the school grounds to ensure that Maria would always have the purest milk. When it came to clothes she made Maria wear loose-fitting Greek tunics and sandals instead of the school uniform to make sure she had enough air circulating around her body.

Even after Maria was married she couldn't escape her mother's interference. The Comtesse insisted that all the trees near Maria's house were cut down – in case she caught something from the bark. While she was pregnant, her mother also made sure that Maria only drank water that had been used to boil pine branches.

When the Comtesse died, her influence was still inescapable. Her will stated that Maria would only be eligible for her share of the fortune if she wore only white in the summer – and never wore lace-up shoes.

When his father died in 1770, William Beckford inherited £1 million in cash along with an income of £100,000 a year – an unbelievable sum for the eighteenth century. It made him the richest ten-year-old boy in England.

He spent most of his youth travelling, accompanied by his doctor, valet, cook and baker plus three footmen, twenty-four musicians, an ugly Spanish dwarf who ate only mushrooms and two dogs named Mrs Fry and Viscount Fartleberry. He insisted that everything was 'just so' and on one trip to Portugal, took a flock of sheep with him just so they could improve the view from his balcony. He also took his own wallpaper so that each room he stayed in could be decorated to his taste.

Beckford returned home in 1795 after a short marriage and a scandal involving a 'handsome young boy'. Back at the family estate at Fonthill in Wiltshire, he cut himself off from society and used his vast wealth to construct a Gothic abbey, a private folly with a mighty tower as its main feature. He had long boasted that he intended to live in the tallest private residence in England – no matter how much it cost.

Before work started he had a huge wall built around his estate to keep out nosy sightseers. This was seven miles long and twelve feet high. Beckford might have had grand schemes but the trait which let him down was his impatience. For a start, he would not wait for proper foundations to be dug, despite the protests of both the architect and the builders. To make sure the tower was built as quickly as possible he used timber and cement rather than the more laborious brick and stone.

During its construction he employed 500 labourers in two shifts, using extra ale rations as an incentive to work faster. He also commandeered every cart in the district to transport building materials, causing farming in the area to be brought to a standstill. Eventually, six years later, the tower was complete. At 275 feet high, it competed with the spire of nearby Salisbury Cathedral – until it crashed to the ground with an ear–splitting roar at the first strong gust of wind.

This didn't seem to faze Beckford and he immediately ordered another tower to be built on the spot – although this would be built from stone. Beckford had the time and the money so he could wait. Seven years later it was completed; only to come down again in a strong gale.

Beckford later moved to Bath where he built a smaller tower, only 150 feet high. He lived to enjoy it for twenty years, dying in 1844 aged eighty-four. This tower, however, has stood the test of time.

In his day, studio boss Sam Goldwyn (the 'G' in MGM) was one of the richest men in Hollywood. Not bad for a barely educated, ex-glove salesman from Minsk originally called Samuel Goldfish. Unfortunately he was also famous for his meanness, his lack of tact and his unique ability to mangle the English language. A number of famous 'Goldwynisms' have now passed into legend. They include:

— This business is dog-eat-dog and nobody is gonna eat me

— The trouble with this business is the dearth of bad pictures

— I don't want any yes men around me. I want everyone to tell me the truth even if it costs them their jobs!

— I'll write you a blanket cheque

— Why call him Joe? Every Tom, Dick and Harry is called Joe!

— I don't think anybody should write his autobiography until after he's dead

— It's more than magnificent – it's mediocre!

— Let's have some new clichés!

— I'll give you a definite maybe

— He's living beyond his means – but he can afford it

— Let's bring it up to date with some snappy nineteenth-century dialogue

— I had a great idea this morning, but I didn't like it

— A verbal contract's not worth the paper it's written on

— I was on the brink of an abscess

— You've bitten the hand of the goose that laid the golden egg

— Include me out

— Anyone who has to see a psychiatrist needs his head examined

— In two words, 'impossible'

— What we want is a story that starts with an earthquake and works its way up to a climax

— Too caustic? To hell with the cost! We'll make the picture anyway!

To many, Goldwyn was the epitome of bad taste. Distressed to learn that there were only twelve disciples in the Bible, Goldwyn thought this jeopardised his latest biblical epic. 'Why only twelve disciples?' he yelled. 'Go out and get thousands!'

When Madam Chiang Kai Shek, wife of the late president of Taiwan, visited MGM studios in the 1930s, Goldwyn greeted her with the words, 'I guess I should have brought along my laundry.'

A few years later he was playing tennis doubles against the king of Siam, and was heard on several occasions urging his partner to 'hit it harder to the Chink'.

The cream of American society were shocked into stunned silence when, in 1702, they were invited to meet the new Governor of New York & New Jersey who had freshly arrived from London.

Before them stood Lord Cornbury – wearing a woman's dress, full make-up, high-heeled satin shoes, a tiara and a bouffant wig, impatiently flicking a delicate lady's lace fan in front of his stubbled face. Before long, silence gave way to titters but an angry scowl from Cornbury silenced them: 'You're all very stupid people!' he chided. 'I represent a Queen, so why shouldn't I dress like one?'

There were many, many good reasons. Not least of which was that Lord Cornbury was a big, strapping, hairy bloke who could never, ever be mistaken for a woman, despite obviously wearing stays in a pathetic attempt to give himself an hourglass figure.

Regardless of the obvious distaste for his appearance and demeanour, Lord Cornbury held his ground and continued to attend all State functions in lady's clothing. He'd had lots of practice – he'd been regularly wearing dresses since the age of eight. He further made himself unpopular by arbitrarily taxing

LORD AND LADY CORNBURY

all Americans for wearing wigs, charging people to attend their own State functions and insisting on being addressed as 'Your High Mightiness'.

His unpopularity only grew when he was caught sneaking up behind a night watchman and goosing him. Surprisingly, perhaps, Lord Cornbury was married, but, less surprisingly, treated his wife like dirt. He ignored her and gave her so little money that she was reduced to stealing food just to survive. When he appeared at her funeral clad in one of her old evening dresses even his few supporters began to desert him and he became universally loathed and detested. Indeed, some historians think that the movement for American independence began at about this time.

£ Lady Cardigan was a wealthy eccentric who caused quite a stir in polite Victorian society. She smoked like a chimney, wore a leopardskin cape and red military trousers when she cycled and would go for walks in Hyde Park wearing a Louis XVI coat and a three-cornered hat. Oh yes, and she kept a coffin in her house and regularly tried it out for size and comfort.

> For reasons best known only to himself, Billy Crystal ripped out a bathroom in his house and had it turned into an exact replica of an aircraft toilet, complete with sickbags.

You remember that at the beginning of this chapter I said, 'Some people appear to have a lot more money than sense ...'? Now do you see what I mean?

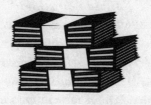

Chapter 9

NOTHING SUCCEEDS LIKE EXCESS

The following conversation is reported to have taken place at the home of Alfred Rothschild:

Butler: *Tea or coffee, sir?*
Guest: *Tea, please.*
Butler: *China, Ceylon or Indian, sir?*
Guest: *China, please.*
Butler: *Lemon, milk or cream, sir?*
Guest: *Milk, please.*
Butler: *Jersey, Hereford or Shorthorn, sir...?*

For some people, once they've got enough money they can't wait to flaunt it. In other cases, they amass such huge fortunes it really is impossible for them to spend it all in a remotely sensible way, so they become more and more ostentatious. Many of the world's multi-millionaires are known to be very, very flash with their cash.

For example, the Sultan of Brunei, not a man particularly known for his thriftiness, spent $25 million – as you do – to celebrate his fiftieth birthday in 1996. He is reported to have at least 150 Rolls-Royces. He also owns the largest residential palace in the world. Completed in 1984, it cost him around $460 million to build and has 1788 rooms, including 257 toilets. So no one staying with the Sultan and his family should ever get caught short.

For one of his son's birthdays, rather than hiring 'Uncle Happy – Balloon Folder Extraordinaire', the Sultan arranged, for an undisclosed but very large sum of money, for Sting to keep his kids amused for a few hours. The Sultan's current wealth is estimated to be around the £22 billion mark.

And Alan J. Lerner and Frederick Lowe wrote a string of smash hit musicals, including *My Fair Lady*, *Gigi* and *Camelot*, which brought them so much money they really didn't know what to do with it. While on a shopping trip to London, the pair of them walked into a Rolls-Royce dealership in Mayfair and ordered identical Rolls-Royce convertibles. As Lerner reached for his cheque book, Lowe indicated for him to please put it away – 'I'll get this,' he said. 'You just got lunch.'

. Madonna once bought a $7,500 diamond-studded choker from Tiffany's. Nothing wrong with that you might think – but it was for her pet Chihuahua, Chiquita.

£ For £3,000 you can get a sex change for your pet at a clinic in California. Apparently it's quite common because, in the words of one sex–change vet: 'Like humans, pets can find themselves trapped in the bodies of the opposite sex.'

Er, yes, of course they do …

£. Guests staying at The Breakers, the summer home of Cornelius Vanderbilt II in Newport, Rhode Island, were spoilt for choice when it came to having a bath. The taps dispensed either fresh water or salt water.

> **When ice skater John Curry met a heavily bejewelled Liberace in 1977, he said, 'You've got so much ice on your hands I could skate on them!'**

£. Aristotle Onassis's ship, the *Christina* – named for his daughter – was in its day one of the most amazing sights on the seas. A 1,700-ton yacht converted from a Canadian frigate, the ship offered him and his guests the ultimate in luxury. The bathrooms were all of sienna marble with solid gold taps, while the stateroom's vast open fireplace was decorated with lapis lazuli. Connecting doors were made of antique Japanese lacquers and the walls were decorated with exquisite Russian icons and two paintings by El Greco. Strangest of all, the bar stools were covered with the scrotums of sperm whales.

Topside, the ship boasted a vast swimming pool and a raised dance floor. The *Christina* also came complete with its own seaplane and eight speedboats.

Don't ask what the price was – but simply maintaining it cost Onassis $1.5 million a year.

£ A burglar who broke into a millionaire's vast Bel Air mansion in June 1982 panicked when he couldn't find the way out. He became thoroughly lost in a maze of indoor swimming pools, indoor tennis courts, enclosed patio, gymnasium, library, art gallery, jacuzzi enclosure, kitchens, balconies and staircases both normal and spiral. After finding himself in the master bedroom, he woke up the owners and begged them to show him the way out. They dutifully arranged for a police escort ...

Greta Garbo once owned the whole of Rodeo Drive, one of the most prestigious streets in all Los Angeles.

£ In 1997, Mick Fleetwood, drummer with Fleetwood Mac, estimated that he'd spent $8 million on cocaine.

£. For a cool million dollars you can have yourself mummified – just like the ancient Egyptian Pharaohs. Well, quite like them. The Egyptians used to prepare bodies for mummification by scraping out the brain with a sharp hook stuck up the nose, but fortunately medical science has moved on since then. The Summum Corporation in Salt Lake City will cover you in a secret formula of preservatives, herbs and white wine, then bandage you up and wedge you inside an airtight sarcophagus. A million dollars gets you the full treatment, but prices can start as low as $7,500 if you just want to preserve a bit of yourself ...

£ When sixty-four-year-old coffee millionaire Antonio Helmut Varboza married his twenty-four-year-old model bride Rita de Recife in Brazil in 1970 the celebrations cost him £445,000! 800 guests ate their way through thirty-seven complete wedding cakes and drank over 100 gallons of champagne. Three years later they got divorced. I wonder what that cost him ...

> **Jurassic Park cost $60 million to make – but $68 million to promote.**

. Do you know where the United States' entire supply of gold leaf went to in 1924? Onto the gilded ceilings of Marjorie Merriwether Post's 115-room mansion in Palm Beach. Work on the ceilings had to be halted while fresh supplies of gold leaf were imported from Europe.

(Incidentally, the house was bought by Donald Trump in 1985 for $10 million – and it costs $3 million a year to maintain.)

Neil Diamond used to bite his fingernails constantly. He didn't want anyone to know so, no matter where he was, he flew his personal manicurist in from Los Angeles to make them presentable before each show.

> **'If you can count your money, you're not seriously rich.'**
> **– Jean Paul Getty**

. Less than twenty-four hours after inheriting £20 million, Stuart Holzman of Florida was to be seen driving a brand new speedboat around Bimini Marina, accompanied by four naked glamour models. The women were reportedly throwing $100 bills over the side of the boat as it sped about.

'My uncle insisted on my having a responsible job until I was thirty-five,' Stuart told a gaggle of reporters later. 'For fifteen years, I've been a rodent infestation officer. Yesterday was my thirty-fifth birthday and I hope I shall never have to be responsible ever again!'

> **A wealthy Arab sheikh once offered to purchase Diana Dors for twenty-three camels.**

When a new railway line was built annoyingly close to his Michigan mansion, wealthy American industrialist John M. Longyear had the entire sixty-room house dismantled brick by brick and then moved half way across the country to Brookline Massachusetts. Every tree, hedge, shrub and plant in his garden was likewise uprooted and lovingly cared for until they could be replanted on his new estate.

When Jeremiah Carlton inherited a vast fortune from his merchant father on 20 May 1790, the first thing the nineteen-year-old did was to go to bed – and stay there. For the rest of his life, he never did another thing. He just stayed in bed, being washed and attended to by his forty-strong team of servants, for seventy years until he died at the ripe old age of eighty-nine.

The Russian Prince Cherkassy owned a villa in Cannes and employed over forty gardeners to change the flower beds every night, just so he could gaze upon new flowers in the morning.

Until it closed in 1986, the Nova Park Elysée hotel was the most expensive in the world. Guests arriving at the hotel were met personally by the manager with a bottle of champagne and a large bouquet of flowers.
 You could pay $7,000 per night for a suite and, although this included a chauffeur-driven Rolls-Royce for the evening, the price didn't include breakfast.

Even by Hollywood's bizarre standards the life – and death – of producer Don Simpson is a story of incredible excess. Reading the life stories of famous executives like Louis B.

Mayer and Harry Warner, Simpson decided he wanted to be just like them – only badder. Fiercely competitive, Simpson was the kind of man who would – and did – urinate over the tennis net after losing a game.

Co-producer of hit films like *Beverly Hills Cop*, *An Officer and a Gentleman*, *Top Gun*, *Flashdance* and *Days of Thunder* in the 1980s, Simpson found himself to be Hollywood's golden boy. He had so much money he didn't know what to do with it. Correction. He knew exactly what to do with it – spend it all on as many fast cars, fast women and expensive drugs as he could lay his hands on – when he wasn't trying to intimidate scriptwriters by waving loaded machine guns around, and screaming at them about scripts they hadn't even written.

In the evenings he was known to employ up to twelve $1,000-a-night hookers at his $4 million home, to indulge his bizarre and sadistic tastes. He kept a stack of Polaroids of girls he'd slept with on his desk to impress fellow producers, next to his Roladex, labelled 'girls'.

He treated his staff like dirt, blaming them if there was turbulence on any flight he took. If he was staying at a hotel, he would never ring room service himself. Even if they were a continent away, he'd ring his assistants back in the office to call room service for him.

With a passion for customised Mustangs, Corvettes, Porsches and Ferrari Testarossas, in less than a year he wrote off three cars while driving under the influence of drink and drugs. After one accident he tried to shift the blame onto a model he was giving a lift home to. 'You should probably leave town,' he told her. 'I've told everyone you were driving my car.' If she didn't go along with the deception, Simpson told her, 'I'll have someone hurt you. I know people.' Unfortunately for him, so did the model. Her boyfriend was well connected in Italian Mafia circles. Don got a visit – and spent the rest of his life being deathly afraid that someone would take him for a ride.

All the drug-taking contributed to his paranoia and acute mental decline. 'Don was in trouble with drugs before anybody was in trouble with drugs,' admitted one of his closest friends. At one time, he was spending $75,000 a month on prescription drugs alone, wolfing down Atarax, Benadryl, Compazine, Venlafaxine, Haldol, Toradol, Librium, Valium, Depakote, Thorazine, Cogetin, Colanadine, Vicodin, Diphenhydramine, Xanax, Phenobarbital, Atarax, Unisom, Nystatin, Lithium carbonate, Narcan, Phenergan, Ativan, Desyrel, Morphine, Seconal, Gamma hydroxybutyrate and Tigan. He was also ingesting huge quantities of alcohol, cocaine and heroin – as well as peanut butter.

He spent £5,900 on a penis widening and lengthening operation performed by top Hollywood practitioner Dr Melvyn

Rosenstein – known to all in the business as 'Dr Dick' – which only left him with a severe infection and violent bruising. He also had a number of face lifts, collagen injections, 'buttock lifts' and testosterone capsules implanted in his bottom to raise his sex drive. Unfortunately, they exploded in his buttocks on the set of *Days of Thunder*, turning him into Hollywood's answer to The Incredible Hulk. He ripped the door off a car with his bare hands and went completely bananas.

Not surprisingly his lifestyle killed him. He died on the toilet on 19 January 1996 while reading a biography of Oliver Stone …

The largest private residence in the United States is a 250-room mansion belonging to George Washington Vanderbilt III. It's in Asheville, North Carolina, and is set in 130,000 acres. At one time, more foresters were employed on site than worked for the entire US Department of Agriculture.

. While staying in the Penthouse Suite at the Desert Inn, Las Vegas, Howard Hughes whiled away the time by trying all thirty-one of Baskin-Robbins' famous ice-cream flavours. After much deliberation, he decided 'Banana Nut' flavour was best and thereafter had two scoops of it with every meal. For several months all went well – until an aide tried to replenish their stocks and found that Baskin-Robbins had discontinued the flavour. There was pandemonium in the Hughes camp. No one knew what the boss would do if he heard his favourite ice cream was being scrapped. Heads would roll for sure. His aides pleaded with Baskin-Robbins to produce more. They said it was possible – but the minimum order was 350 gallons. In desperation, the aides agreed.

They rearranged all the food storage freezers in the Desert Inn kitchens, then personally drove down to Los Angeles to supervise the lorry delivery, smuggling it in at the dead of night so that their boss wouldn't suspect anything was wrong. The very next day, after Hughes had finished his traditional scoops of 'Banana Nut', he turned to his aides and said, 'That's great ice cream – but it's time for a change. From now on I want French Vanilla …'

£ Charlie Sheen once spent $6,537 to buy all 2,615 seats in an area of his favourite baseball stadium, just so he could sit there alone and have more chance of catching a home run ball. Sad … or what?

> **Catherine de' Medici had a dress especially made for her, studded with 3,000 diamonds and 39,000 pearls. She only ever wore it once.**

£ **So that she didn't have to waste any of her valuable time trying on different outfits, millionairess Eva Stotebury kept a fashion artist on staff at her Philadelphia mansion. The artist would sketch her employer wearing the different combinations she chose, then show these to her for her approval.**

£. Fred Astaire once described Hollywood as 'the place where you spend more than you earn, on things you don't need, to impress people you don't like'.

£ The eccentric British millionaire the fourth Marquis of Blandford once offered the Countess di Castiglione one million francs for a night of passion. The countess had previously been the mistress of Emperor Napoleon III of France, who had given her a necklace worth half a million francs, and King Victor

Emmanuel II of Sardinia as well as Baron James de Rothschild and his three sons.

The Countess accepted the Marquis's offer and, by all accounts, she really earned her million. She was physically incapable of getting out of bed for three days afterwards!

The Countess started to go mad at the age of forty, driven to despair by her fading looks. She drew the blinds in her apartment, covered up all the mirrors and spent her remaining days trying to teach her two pet dogs to do a waltz ...

. When Harrods installed Britain's first ever escalator in 1898, the top people's store employed liveried attendants to hand out smelling salts and brandy to customers brave enough to risk the journey!

Archduke Francis Ferdinand of Austria was so vain that he insisted he was tightly sewn into his clothes every morning to avoid creases. When he was shot, in Sarajevo in 1914, the doctors couldn't get his clothes off to get to the wound – and so he bled to death. His assassination sparked the First World War.

. André Citröen always thought big when it came to publicising his car company. During the Paris Exposition in 1922 he hired a skywriting aeroplane to spell his name out above the crowds, while visitors were given free rides to the show in Citröen courtesy cars.

Outdoing the aeroplane stunt, he later persuaded the Governors of Paris to fit 36,000 light bulbs to the Eiffel Tower spelling out his name. One of his other publicity-grabbing events was a little more bizarre – constantly losing large sums of money at the gambling tables just so he could hit the headlines.

Sadly his love of gambling (and losing, it seems) got the better of the multi-millionaire and he frittered his fortune away in this manner, dying broke.

The billionaire with the grandest name of all time must surely be the German Prince Albert Maria Lamoral Miguel Johannes Gabriel von Thurn und Taxis. His fortune is estimated to be in the region of $3 billion and he lives in a 500-room Bavarian palace, attended by seventy servants. It is said that when he was younger he came home confused from school one day, asking his mother why one of his school friends didn't have an original Rembrandt, like they did.

. King Richard II is sometimes credited with inventing the handkerchief. Because of his habit of having regular baths and reading books, everyone assumed he was gay – which was right on the money, as it happens. Fed up with all the butch war stories being told about his dad, the so-called Black Prince, Richard tried to make the court a more aesthetically pleasing place, full of fashion and art. Instead, he just fuelled a fashion for ridiculous excess.

Courtiers wore their sleeves so long they trailed along the ground after them. Their shoes were so long and pointed that they had to be rolled up and tied to the knee to stop the wearer falling over, and Richard himself spent over a thousand pounds on a beautiful gem-encrusted party dress. He also threw a Christmas party for 10,000 guests and spent tens of thousands of pounds on jewels to put in his boyfriend's coffin.

> **'Cocaine is God's way of saying you're making too much money.'**
> **– Robin Williams**

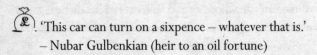

'This car can turn on a sixpence – whatever that is.'
– Nubar Gulbenkian (heir to an oil fortune)

In 1930, Babe Ruth earned a huge salary of $80,000 a year (today that would be the equivalent of over $900,000). In addition to his salary, Ruth earned lucrative bonuses and personal-appearance fees, boosting his income to over $3 million in today's terms. He once purchased an entire St Louis brothel for the night …

'I totally appreciate being able to buy, say, this thousand-dollar cashmere blanket – because if I couldn't, I would hate the fact that I would have to go back to real, regular blankets.'
– Stevie Nicks (Fleetwood Mac)

When millionaire rap star Ice-T was offered $500 a day for his role in the film, *Breakin'* he was not impressed, pointing out that he spent that much on a pair of sneakers.

Andrew Lloyd Webber made £3.5 million when he sold his wine collection. One bottle of Chateau Lafitte fetched £105,000.

Eighteen-year-old golf fanatic Aaron Howard from Perthshire, Scotland, was pleased when his mother, Heather, said she was going to buy him a golf club. The club she had in mind, however, wasn't a four iron – but a £4 million championship golf course at El Bosque, near Valencia in Spain, that's been played by stars including Ian Woosnam and José Maria Olazabal.

Wealthy businesswoman Heather first visited the course while in Spain last year. She heard it was for sale and, in her own words, 'took the plunge and bought it'. She hopes that one day, Aaron will become El Bosque's touring professional. How did Aaron react when he heard about his gift? Well he was shocked, but has since vowed 'to do anything I can to pay her back' – including lots of practice.

It took just eight punches for world heavyweight champ Mike Tyson to finish off his opponent Michael Spinks in Atlantic City in 1988. His earnings from the fight worked out at a staggering $2.5 million per punch.

But that was nothing for Tyson. In 1997 alone he made $75 million and got himself into the record books as the highest-paid athlete in the history of sport. He would have earned even more in 1998 if he hadn't decided to bite a few lumps out of Evander Holyfield's ear.

. There might be some truth in the myth that the best way to drink champagne is from a lady's shoe. An American chemist, Russell Erb, claims that because the leather of the shoe is nitrogenous, it accentuates the flavour and aroma of the drink.

Elton John once spent $850,000 on a single day's shopping spree. One of his associates later said about Elton, 'When the going gets tough, the tough go shopping.'

. David Lee Roth, the ex-lead singer of Van Halen, might have been a flamboyant performer but he could also be a real prima donna at times.

Backstage before a concert in Pueblo, Colorado, he noticed a bowl of M&Ms on the buffet table, including (shock, horror!) some brown ones. According to Roth, brown M&Ms were expressly banned under the terms of the group's contract. To show his anger at this blatant disregard of a legal document Roth kicked over the buffet table, wrecked the whole of the backstage area and kicked a large hole in a wall.

When presented with a large bill for all the damage Roth later commented, 'I'm prepared to pay that to have a good time.'

Roth's idea of a good time also included his road manager pouring Perrier water over his aching feet after a concert.

What did Alva Vanderbilt receive for a birthday present from her husband William in 1892? A mansion named Marble House that cost $2 million to build – and $9 million to decorate and furnish.

This fifty-room palace at Newport, Rhode Island was modelled on the White House. Features included a $75,000 fireplace with a mantel from Pompeii, bronze and steel front doors that weighed a ton and a half each and original Gothic stained–glass windows.

While most women would have appreciated William's generosity, it wasn't enough for Alva. She left him four years later for another millionaire, Oliver H. P. Belmont. His mansion, Belcourt, cost $3 million to build and had sixty rooms. He kept thirteen horses in the grounds – and two stuffed ones in the house.

> **'Whoever said money can't buy happiness didn't know where to shop.'**
> **– Gittel Hudnick**

Paul Cravath, a rich American lawyer, built a huge estate on Long Island and asked his architect if he could incorporate a running brook in the drawing room.

The architect sarcastically replied, 'Would that be a brook that babbles or one that burbles?'

'Both,' said Mr Cravath.

The brook was duly installed as per his wishes.

TV producer Aaron Spelling's mansion in Beverly Hills is built on the site of Bing Crosby's former home. Among its 120 rooms is a fifty-seat cinema, a full-size bowling alley and a windowless room with its own independent air supply in case of terrorist attack.

Rock band Aerosmith are noted for their extravagances. On their first British tour they rented a forty-seat private plane at a cost of £18,000 per day. At the time the band was only earning £3,000 per show …

In those early days, money also had to be set aside for

paying for wrecked hotel rooms. Equipment taken on tour expressly for this purpose included a chainsaw and extra-long extension leads. These were so the TVs that were thrown out of hotel windows would keep playing all the way down to the ground.

At a stadium show in Toronto in the late 1970s the band members travelled from their dressing rooms to the stage in limousines – a distance of a hundred yards.

When it came to recording, nothing was too much trouble to get the sound they wanted. The band were having dinner together when someone put on 'You See Me Crying' from their 1975 album *Toys In The Attic*. Vocalist Steve Tyler thought it was great: 'We gotta cover this!' he shouted. 'Who is it?'

Guitarist Joe Perry replied, 'It's us, f***head. Who the f*** do you think it is? It's that song you made us hire a 109-piece orchestra for!'

When Brian Wilson, vocalist with the Beach Boys, needed a little inspiration he had the floor of his den, where his piano was located, completed covered in sand.

Steve Ross, the former Time Warner chief, once flew his wife and four friends to Mexico for Christmas. He took two executive planes – one for the people and one for the gifts.

Not many people can claim to have a volcano in their back garden but the late millionaire financier Sir James Goldsmith was one. His estate in Careyes, Mexico, had an active volcano within its 40,000 acres.

It also had its own police force and staff whose only job was to kill scorpions.

> **Donald Trump's private Boeing 727 had gold–plated seat belt buckles.**

How much would you spend on your daughter's twenty-first birthday party? £100? £200? £500?

To celebrate his daughter Alana's twenty-first, Galen Weston, chief executive of a chain of Canadian supermarkets, was reported to have spent £250,000 in 1993 – but then he could afford it; he was then estimated to be worth over £600 million.

£ On one of their travels across Europe, Edward and Mrs Simpson took with them 220 suitcases. They probably didn't manage to sneak through with it all as hand luggage, then ...

. When Donald and Ivana Trump were divorced she received $10 million in cash, a $4 million housing allowance, $100,000 per year for each of their three children and their forty-five-room house in Connecticut.

That's nothing though, compared to what Anne, wife of the Texan billionaire Sid Bass, received in their divorce in 1988. Her settlement is reported to have been worth $300 million.

£ There's parties and there's parties. For his seventieth birthday in 1989, magazine publisher Malcolm S. Forbes flew 700 colleagues and friends to Tangiers on board a 747, a DC-8 and Concorde. 200 waiters were on hand to wash the guests' hands before they ate and the entertainment include precision drilling from the 270-man Moroccan Cavalry. The cost was estimated at $2 million.

But that pales into insignificance when you consider the Shah of Iran's 1971 party to celebrate the

2,500th anniversary of the founding of the Persian Empire. The food came from Maxims in Paris, who flew over 1,590 chefs to Iran to prepare it. The whole shindig took place in sixty air-conditioned marquees and cost in the region of $100 million.

. Frederick the Great of Prussia is said to have had his coffee brewed with champagne rather than with water.

In 1997 wealthy Raymond Orton took revenge on his ex–wife following the break-up of his marriage by withdrawing £100,000 in cash from their joint account and burning it in the back garden of his Birmingham home.

. In the 1930s the American millionaire Frank Gould took a ten–piece band with him whenever he went on holiday so that he could always hear his favourite songs.

By the time Ross Perot bought his childhood home in Texarkana, the bricks had all been painted white. Wanting to restore its appearance, he arranged for them all to be sandblasted. The paint was so old, however, that it could not be removed. Not one to give up easily, Perot then ordered his house taken to pieces and then rebuilt brick by brick – with the bricks turned around so that the unpainted sides faced the street.

. 'Anyone who thinks greed is a bad thing, I want to tell you it's not a bad thing. And I think that in our system, everybody should be a little bit greedy ... You shouldn't feel guilty.'
   – Ivan Boesky, Wall Street trader before his three-year prison sentence and $100 million fine for insider trading.

Imelda Marcos, wife of Filipino dictator President Marcos, has been called everything from the 'Iron Lady' to 'Blood Sucker' – and probably far worse. When she and her husband were forced to flee to Hawaii after a coup broke out, she didn't have time to pack the usual 400 bags that accompanied her on trips abroad. Instead, she had just time to fill a single suitcase with the little things that meant the most to her – like handfuls of bank notes, a gold crown studded with diamonds, three tiaras, an emerald brooch worth $1 million, sixty pearl necklaces, sixty-five gold watches and thirty-five expensive rings.

Among the possessions she was forced to leave behind were 3,000 pairs of shoes, 2,000 dresses, 35 racks of furs, 500 black bras, one bulletproof bra, 200 St Michael girdles, 1,500 handbags, vats of French perfumes and hundreds of bars of exclusive French soaps. She was also forced to leave behind her favourite pair of dancing shoes, which had special flashing disco lights built into the heels.

Many of her possessions had been accumulated during fabulous spending sprees. Congressman Stephen Solarz of New York commented, 'She made Marie Antoinette look like a bag lady.' On one spree alone, it's estimated that she spent $6.5 million of her country's money. In one single afternoon's shopping in New York she once bought $330,000 worth of jewellery. If she liked an item of clothing or a pair of shoes, she would buy ten dozen – and if she wasn't certain, she would only buy five dozen.

Imelda was never embarrassed about her wealth and possessions. She believed she was entitled to it – and to run her country – by divine right. She despised Cory Aquino, who became the Philippines' new president after the coup, and said that she could never be a good president 'because she doesn't make up or do her nails'.

Even in the early days of Hollywood, they knew how to spend money like water. In 1933, when Cecil B. De Mille was planning to make *Cleopatra*, he sent an expedition to Egypt to study the colour of the Pyramids. The expedition studied ninety-two major and lesser pyramids, cost over $100,000 and reported back that the pyramids were indeed sandy brown – just as De Mille had thought. What the famous director intended to do with this costly information isn't known – as he made *Cleopatra* in black and white!

In the 1980s, Adnan Mohamed Khashoggi was worth between an estimated $2–4 billion, a fabulous wealth accumulated by acting as a dealer, consultant and middleman in everything from arms to oil. His pride and joy was his 282-foot custom-built yacht the *Nabila*. The yacht, which cost him $70 million (just over half of what Khashoggi would spend in an average year) featured its own disco, cinema, helicopter and landing pad, medical operating room, swimming pool and communications centre, as well as eight staterooms, six guests suites each named after precious stones and a dining room for sixteen. The upper deck, which was rarely without a flock of bikini-clad starlets, was protected by sheets of bulletproof glass. The boat was hired by Hollywood to appear in the James Bond adventure *Never Say Never Again*.

Even more spectacular than the boat itself were the parties Khashoggi would throw on it for movie stars, royalty and other members of the jet set. Sadly, he believed in all honesty that only two out of every ten of his friends would still speak to him if he had no money …

Before he finally sold the yacht to Donald Trump, Khashoggi announced ambitious plans for further improvements. These include facilities to berth his seven-man mini submarine, his-and-her helicopter pads, garaging for four Rolls-Royces and a battery of surface-to-air missiles.

'Nothing succeeds like excess,' said Liberace – and he should know. Although a consummate pianist, the real secret of his success was his sheer showmanship. People came to see him as much as they came to hear him. His rhinestone-and-sequin-covered costumes were extravaganzas in themselves – some of them took a year to make. When people wondered how he could play the piano with the weight of the diamond-encrusted gold rings that were as much a part of his trademark as his gold candelabra he replied, 'Very well, thank you!'

Liberace lived a life of excess off stage as well as on. His Beverly Hills mansion featured a piano-shaped swimming pool and a collection of rare Rolls-Royces. Not bad for a boy from Milwaukee whose father wanted him to be an undertaker!

Described as 'the heart-throb of forty million women', the Daily Mirror was less than impressed with the entertainer's sex appeal. They described him as, among other things, a 'fruit-flavoured, mincing, ice-covered heap of mother love, the biggest sentimental vomit of all time' and 'a calculating candy floss'. At the libel trial that followed (and which they lost), they argued Fair Comment.

Even after his death his larger-than-life legend lives on. On 10 February 1989 a large number of witnesses in the town of Fyffe, Alabama, claimed they had seen Liberace – now twelve foot tall – step out of a golden, banana-shaped UFO and play a medley of showstoppers on a floating giant grand piano.

£ **Joseph Pulitzer wanted a little bit of peace and quiet in his Fifth Avenue mansion – so he had it soundproofed with $2 million worth of additional marble.**

Motor manufacturer Ettore Bugatti was accosted at a 1927 cocktail party by a slightly drunk English woman who said, 'You undoubtedly make fine automobiles, Signor Bugatti, but I am afraid that the Rolls-Royce is still the finest.'

That remark hurt Bugatti's pride so much that he immediately set about designing a new car to outRolls a Rolls. What he came up with was the Type 41, or 'Bugatti Royale' as it's more commonly known. Only six were built between 1927 and 1939. Each luxury car was twenty-two feet long and powered by a 12.7 litre eight-cylinder engine and guaranteed for life. Bugatti screened prospective owners and paid special attention to their pedigrees – the only people eligible to buy one were bona fide kings or princes. No one else was permitted, regardless of how wealthy they were.

At the time the cars sold for $55,000. Believe it or not all six cars are still running today and have proved to be an excellent investment. In 1990, one of the cars was bought by a Japanese corporation for $10 million.

> 'A billion here, a billion there – pretty soon it adds up to real money.'
> – Senator Everett Dirksen

Chapter 10

ONE BRIGHT IDEA

Writing for a penny a word is ridiculous. If a man really wants to make a million, the best way would be to start a religion.
— *L. Ron Hubbard, founder of Scientology (and ex-pulp fiction writer)*

Some people inherit huge amounts of money, although their number is getting smaller and smaller every year. Some people build up huge companies and amass their fortune that way. And others just have the one right, bright idea at the right time and just a few seconds of genius sets them and their families up for ever.

Like Yorkshireman Percy Shaw, who became a millionaire many times over – and all because he had trouble finding his way back from the pub in the fog. This meant negotiating a dark, winding road with a sheer drop on one side. One night in 1930 he was cautiously negotiating the bend when his car headlamps picked up two small but bright points of light. These were the eyes of a black cat that was sitting by the side of the road.

Realising he had the solution, Percy went into business and he made his first cat's eyes road reflectors in 1934 and soon had a factory manufacturing 30,000 pairs a week. It's estimated that he earned more than £10 million from this one invention but Percy continued to live in the same house he'd lived in all his life. He refused to have curtains because they obscured the view; likewise with carpets so that he could toss discarded matches he used to light his pipe straight onto the floor. His pipe, by the way, was

always filled with crushed-up cigars. His one real extravagance was that much later in life he bought three televisions, which he left permanently on, tuned to three different channels.

Every 2.3 seconds a Tupperware party begins somewhere in the world. What a revolting thought! This sad symbol of suburbia takes its name from its inventor. No, there wasn't a Mr Tupperware, but there was an Earl S. Tupper, a chemist who worked at Du Pont in the 1930s. He always dreamed of creating his own range of stylish but practical food containers but plastics were in their infancy and there was no suitable material. The breakthrough came in 1942 with the invention of polyethylene, a much more flexible, softer and hard-wearing plastic. Because of the war, though, he couldn't obtain the raw material so he used to take home with him bags of discarded petroleum waste from Du Pont.

The first product he made at home was a bathroom drinking tumbler available in a range of colours but, by 1947, he'd also developed his famous lidded bowls that would make him a multi-millionaire. These were originally known as his 'Poly-T Wonder Bowls' and although they had good reviews at the time, they didn't sell that well in the shops. Tupper realised that customers needed to see the products in action, so he devised his now famous home party system, run by Tupperware Hostesses. This was a brilliant marketing ploy and by the third year in business he'd topped $25 million in sales. In a few decades these parties were selling over $900 million worth of Tupperware ...

I'm sure you'll be interested to learn that there was even an official Tupperware song, which used to be sung at all the best Tupperware parties. It went:

I've got that Tupperware feeling deep in my heart
Deep in my heart (Where?)
Deep in my heart (Where?)
Deep in my heart
I've got that Tupperware feeling deep in my heart
Deep in my heart to stay.

Finally, let me tell you about a little sales trick that Tupper invented. Tupperware provide pencils for customers to fill in their order forms – but they don't have rubbers attached. This makes it difficult for customers to change their minds.

Having devised a unique product and a unique way of selling it, Tupper retired in 1958, selling his company for approximately $9 million.

Sylvester Stallone was down to his last $100 – and had a pregnant wife to support – when he wrote *Rocky*. His career at that time mainly consisted of 'now you see him, now you don't' appearances in films like *Cannonball* and *Death Race 2000*. He'd also made a porno movie. Several studios liked the screenplay for *Rocky*, but weren't remotely interested in Stallone playing the lead role, which he insisted he must. In the end he virtually gave the screenplay away – on the condition that he played Rocky and shared handsomely in the profits if the film was a hit. It was, and all Stallone's money worries were behind him … He's now worth at least £200 million!

Ever bought a Beanie Baby and wondered what the letters 'TY' stood for on the tag?

It's the name of the inventor of this multi-billion-dollar line of toys, a Mr H. Ty Warner, one of the richest tycoons in the world.

The Beanie Babies were first launched at a Toy Fair in 1993 and have since become one of the most successful toys in the world. The brains behind the Beanie Babies craze is an intensely private man and considered by many to be a marketing genius. Not a lot is known about him. He doesn't give interviews, isn't seen in public and forbids employees giving out any information on his private life. All that is known about him is that he's in his fifties and used to work as a salesman and designer for the toy manufacturer Dakin, selling stuffed animals to speciality shops. He left Dakin in 1980, worked in Italy for a while and then got back into the soft toy business when he founded Ty Inc. in 1985, manufacturing a range of stuffed cats he designed himself.

The Beanie Babies' unbelievable worldwide success is based on Ty's practice of constantly introducing new characters in the range, at the same time as retiring older ones, creating instant collectors' items and triggering a buying frenzy among both adults and children.

Ty Inc, his company, is privately owned and is almost as secretive as he is. Based in a Chicago suburb, there is no sign up, the address is a PO Box number, it doesn't advertise and refuses to give out its phone number. It's said that even the biggest retailers of Beanie Babies can only get hold of Ty executives through an anonymous 800 number which, according to many, is permanently engaged. The demand for the toys is so great that shops have no choice but to stock them – in large quantities – although they're not happy about the power the company wields.

An anonymous New York area gift shop owner told the press: 'They take a high-and-mighty stance. If you place an order you may get something completely different from what you ordered, and you're supposed to be happy to accept it.' The Beanies themselves might be cuddly but Warner's attitude towards competitors is not, having taken out several large lawsuits against companies manufacturing Beanie look-alikes.

Being privately owned, it's difficult to get any accurate

details about the company's turnover or Mr Warner's personal wealth. This year he introduced a very special Beanie Baby that's guaranteed to become the hottest collector's item yet. Only 700–1,000 were manufactured and the tag on each has been personally autographed by Ty. All of his employees were given two to celebrate over $1 billion worth of orders shipped in 1998. The name of this new Beanie? Billionaire Bear.

P.S. They're already on sale on the Internet for upwards of $1,000 each!

It seems you don't have to have invented Beanie Babies in order to make a fortune from them. Husband and wife Sue and Les Fox wrote an unofficial buying guide called 'The Beanie Baby Handbook' in March 1997, investing $100,000 of their six-year-old daughter's college fund to publish it themselves. Book distributors wouldn't touch it so they mailed the major toy and book stores from home.

After a slow start, orders came flooding in at an unbelievable rate. In 1997 they sold one million copies and in 1998, over 1.1 million. The book shop chain Barnes and Noble was selling over 20,000 copies per week! Sue and Les have so far earned an estimated $2 million from the book ...

It's estimated that paparazzi Daniel Angeli and Jean-Paul Dousset earned £2 million just for taking those famous pics of John Bryant sucking Fergie's toes. Another of their other victims, Fiat boss Gianni Agnelli, got so fed up with them chasing him that he went and posed for full-frontal pictures. After that, they gave up ...

In 1819, William K. Clarkson's wife threatened to leave him if he didn't make enough money to buy her 'a proper carriage' to ride around in. The inventor, she said, spent all his money on bits and bobs for inventions which never worked, and she was sick of it. In desperation, Clarkson spent his last $50 on a patent for his latest invention, the 'new improved Curricle'.

Shortly after, Mrs Clarkson had all the money she could ever want as thousands of her husband's inventions started to be sold – under the new name of the 'bicycle'.

In 1885, a photography enthusiast named George Eastman threw in his dull safe job as a bank clerk to pursue his dream. He formed the Eastman Dry Plate and Film Company and within three years had revolutionised the industry by producing a small portable camera which he called the 'Detective Camera', because detectives were in vogue at the time. It had no viewfinder and no focus adjustment and the negatives tended to rip – but it was a breakthrough.

The same year he changed the name of the camera to Kodak – because 'it sounded snappy' (and he wasn't making a pun). Within six years, he sold over 100,000 'Kodaks' and now lived the life of Riley in a thirty-seven-room mansion he shared with his mum …

. There *was* an original Colonel Sanders and he *did* invent a recipe containing eleven different herbs and spices for his fried chicken. However, Colonel Harland Sanders wasn't the one who really benefited from it. A former street car conductor, insurance salesman, tyre salesman, lawyer and farm hand, Harland Sanders had also been a soldier – but there's no evidence he ever rose above the rank of corporal. When he was sixty-five, he settled down to run a small petrol station in Corbin, Kentucky, with a diner attached where he developed his special formula.

When business got tough, the colonel sold out for a million dollars. Restaurateur Leon Harman bought the recipe (and name) from him and went on to create a business which, by the 1960s, was turning over $37 million a year. The Kentucky Fried Chicken Corporation kept in touch and, in 1978, threw a lavish party to celebrate the Colonel's eighty-eighth birthday. They invited 800 guests to their corporate headquarters – for a roast beef meal.

It's been called 'an enigma you can hold in your hand', 'the toy with one moving part' and 'a liquid solid'.

What am I talking about? None other than Silly Putty, an invention that came about when the US Government was looking for a cheaper alternative to rubber during the Second World War. During their experiments, General Electric came up with a strange 'bouncing putty' but no one knew what to do with it. You could make it into a ball, you could stretch it if you pulled it slowly, snap it if you pulled it quickly. It could take impressions of other objects. Oh yes, and it could pick up print from newspapers. And in any case, by 1945 synthetic rubber was by now already being produced and it seemed like this substance didn't have any use whatsoever.

Fun-loving GE scientists (yes, there were some) messed about with the strange material and at a party in 1949, a sample got into the hands of an unemployed advertising executive called Peter Hodgson. As soon as he first fingered the stuff the phrase 'Silly Putty' came to mind. Although he was already $12,000 in debt, he managed to scrape together $147 and bought 21lbs of it, plus the production rights, from General Electric at $7 per pound.

He then packaged the material into little plastic eggs which he sold as an adult toy at an incredible 900% mark-up of $2 per half ounce. These started doing well, with a few outlets selling about 300 eggs per day. Then *New Yorker* magazine featured Silly Putty in a small story and a few days later Peter was inundated with orders for 230,000 eggs!

Since then over 200 million eggs have been sold filled with 3,000 tons of Silly Putty.

The crew of Apollo 8 even used it to secure tools in zero-gravity. Fifty years later Silly Putty is still a recognised name in over ninety-five per cent of American households and remains one of the classic novelty products of modern times. Peter Hodgson, of course, became a multimillionaire from his invention. He died in 1976, leaving an estate worth $140 million.

The great American showman Phineas T. Barnum made his fortune based on one simple philosophy – 'There's one born every minute.' He made millions by exploiting the gullibility of the American public.

Here was the man who drew in the crowds by promising the unusual sight of a 'cherry coloured cat'. When they paid their money, all they got to see was an ordinary black alley cat. 'They were black cherries,' Barnum explained. On another occasion, punters paid a small fortune to see 'a horse whose head is where its tail should be' – only to discover Barnum had put the horse into its stall back to front so that its tail was dangling in its food trough!

One of his most famous hoaxes was the Feejee Mermaid, which he claimed was genuine but which was really half an orang-utan glued on to half a fish. Typically for Barnum, he sold the exclusive story to three newspapers. Despite the fact that Barnum couldn't even spell Fiji properly, tens of thousands of customers paid the (then) not inconsiderable sum of twenty-five cents to see it when it went on display. He also claimed to have the 'Missing Link' in one of his cages – and to have converted him to Christianity.

His greatest triumph, however, was probably his 'discovery' of the woman he presented as 'George Washington's wet nurse'.

The old lady in question was really Joyce Heth, an elderly, toothless black lady in her eighties, whose withered skin made her look a lot, lot older. Barnum billed her as being 161 years old and she was an immediate success. Thousands upon thousands of weeping patriots paid to hear her relate memories of little Georgie and first-hand anecdotes about the Revolutionary War.

Gradually public interest in her declined but Barnum had another trick up his sleeve. Anonymously, he spread rumours via local newspapers that Barnum was a fraud: that Heth wasn't an elderly woman at all – but a robotic impostor. The crowds came flooding back in their thousands to get a second look, and Barnum took great pleasure in 'proving' these scandalous stories wrong!

Another great scam Barnum perpetrated on his customers was to build a door with a big sign on it saying, 'This way to the Egress'. Customers would queue up for ages to go through the door, wondering what an earth an 'egress' could be and curious for a peek. Of course, it was simply a posh way of saying 'way out' and the unfortunates found themselves outside the showground and having to pay to come back in again. Many did – just for the pleasure of watching others queuing to see 'the egress'! Another variation on this was a railway carriage with 'The Great Unknown' written on it – which the paying public discovered was completely empty when they stepped inside.

It's reassuring to know then, that the man who earned over $2 million by circus scams and exhibiting sideshow freaks was himself made bankrupt by another con artist. In 1855, he was persuaded by a con man to invest over half a million dollars in the Jerome Clock Company. It ruined him – but he made an astounding comeback, largely by giving lectures entitled 'How to Make Money'.

The spiteful old bastard also changed his will to leave his daughter Helen a worthless piece of land in Colorado instead of a lifelong stipend, after she left her husband. It turned out, however, that the land was packed with valuable mineral deposits, and Helen ended up richer than all the other Barnum heirs combined.

It's hardly surprising that Dr John Harvey Kellogg was so keen on cereal. After all, he believed that eating meat would turn you into a compulsive masturbator. Armed with sound medical knowledge like this, Kellogg opened his 'Medical Reform Institute' in Battle Creek, Michigan, in 1876 and set about offering some rather startling treatments for even more startled patients. If you looked underweight, Kellogg would have you pinned to your bed by a heavy pile of sandbags and then force-feed you twenty-six meals a day. You weren't allowed to do the slightest thing – even your teeth were cleaned for you to avoid burning up valuable calories. If he couldn't tell what was wrong with you he'd just stick you in a wheelchair and feed you gluten wafers and yoghurt for months on end.

Luckily, Kellogg employed a stringent selection process to screen potential patients – if they were genuinely ill he wouldn't let them anywhere near the place. That way no one would get harmed by his unorthodox treatments. The patients he wanted were wealthy neurotics who would end up being convinced they were cured.

Most of Kellogg's medical breakthroughs occurred to him while he was on the toilet, and he would dictate his new ideas through the door to his assistants. Despite the craziness of it all, Kellogg's 'Temple of Health' attracted many of the wealthiest men of the day, including Teddy Roosevelt and John D. Rockefeller.

When not rewriting medical science, Kellogg had a secret passion to create a flaky breakfast cereal. The correct breakfast cereal would, he believed, be the single biggest medical breakthrough ever achieved in the fight against masturbation.

My God – they don't put that on the packet, do they?

According to his own account, he actually dreamed the formula for corn flakes. Awakening from the dream and still in his night shirt, Kellogg immediately rushed downstairs and knocked off the first batch.

Kellogg's cornflakes proved to be very popular with his patients. One of them, a Mr C. W. Post, realised that Kellogg was a loony – but there was a great future in his breakfast cereal. He fled the sanatorium, started making breakfast cereals like Grape–Nuts and, in no time at all, became one of the wealthiest men in America.

Soon, the whole country had gone stark raving mad over breakfast cereals. By 1900, no less than forty–four companies in the town where Kellogg had his sanatorium were churning out cereals for the nation. People were making absolute fortunes with the most disgusting concoctions, claiming that the worse they tasted, the better that they were for you. One Reverend made up a concoction over breakfast and sold it for $100,000 almost straight away. The day of the 'breakfast barons' was at hand. Some religious groups were quick to condemn this greed. The Seventh-Day Adventists referred to Kellogg's sanatorium as a 'cereal sodom'.

Ironically, Kellogg himself made no money through his cornflakes during this time. He patented his cornflakes as late as 1907. However, they tasted a good deal better than most of the other cereals around and immediately proved popular. But by then, his brother William had secretly bought a majority shareholding in the company and forced John out. Dr Kellogg was incensed and never spoke to his brother again.

Leo Hendrik Baekeland was born in Belgium in 1863. His father was a cobbler, his mother a maid. Inspired by stories of people who made it big in America, Baekeland decided he'd have a go – and succeeded beyond his wildest dreams.

A talented chemist, he invented a new way of developing photographs. Kodak said they were interested, so Baekeland set off to meet Kodak president George Eastman. On the journey, the inventor tried to work out the value of his new process. He decided he'd really like $50,000 dollars for the process but would accept $25,000. During the negotiations, he wisely kept his mouth shut – and came away with a staggering three quarters of a million dollars for his invention.

But Baekeland's greatest achievement was yet to come. In 1907, he patented Bakelite, an early forerunner of plastic. He beat Scotsman James Swinburne to the patent by just twenty-four hours and it made him a multi-millionaire. By all accounts though, as Baekeland got richer, he became more and more withdrawn and miserable. He ended up a miserly old recluse, shut away in his Florida mansion, shunning his family and eating cold food out of tin cans until he died in 1944.

. Dick Tracy was more than just the first police comic strip. It dispensed with the traditional slapstick in favour of extreme violence. Chester Gould, his creator, had learned to draw from a $20 per lesson mail order correspondence school. He was a failure, struggling to keep his family supported, until one day he found the inspiration he had been looking for: 'Everybody was worked up about the hell Chicago gangsters were raising. One day I told myself, "I'm going to draw a guy who'll go out and shoot those sons of bitches!" So I drew six strips around a detective named "Plainclothes Tracy", a real rugged guy.' Gould spent the last of his money on a decent suit and set off to meet Captain Joseph Patterson, head of the *Chicago Tribune*. Patterson suggested 'Dick' as 'Plainclothes' was too long, and encouraged Gould to draw thirty-six strips in just two weeks.

At its height, 100 million people read the strip. President Roosevelt himself would phone up and ask for the solution to the mystery ahead of publication.

In 1979 Canadian friends Scott Abbott and Chris Haney sat down to play Scrabble when they noticed some pieces were missing. Haney went out to buy a new set but was horrified to pay $16 for the privilege. This got them thinking about inventing their own game and various ideas were tossed around until deciding on the key word 'trivia'.

The game and the questions were worked out in less than an hour and the duo offered shares in their new game, now called 'Trivial Pursuit', to friends. Hardly anyone was interested but the small amount of capital they did raise enabled them to market 20,000 games – which sold out in Canada.

Since then over sixty million sets have been sold in thirty–three countries and twenty languages, equal to over $1 billion worth of revenue. Needless to say, Abbott, Haney and their original investors became multimillionaires. How many millions of dollars they've earned is unknown but let's just say, the amount's not trivial …

The game was the inspiration for Robert Angel, a Seattle waiter, to devise Pictionary. For a long time he'd played a version of this with friends but the success of Trivial Pursuit convinced him that he should market it. Soon he'd selected 2,500 words and a colleague had devised the board. By the end of 1987 over $90 million worth of Pictionary games were sold in the US alone.

William Painter was the man who invented flip-off bottle caps. His maxim for success was, 'Invent something people can only use once and then throw away'. In 1895 he explained this theory to one of his salesmen, King Camp Gillette.

Gillette wondered what he could invent and an idea hit him one morning while he was shaving with a cut-throat razor. 'I found my razor not only dull, but beyond the point of successful stropping. As I stood there with the razor in my hand, my eyes resting on it lightly as a bird settling down on its nest, the Gillette razor was born.'

This was the first safety razor, but for years Gillette struggled with making good quality disposable blades. Working with a man named William Nickerson, who devised a wider blade, they developed a successful system in 1903.

When it came to the name, they decided they couldn't call a razor a Nickerson as it was too suggestive of nicked skin. Gillette's name and face went on the wrapper and within a few years he was a millionaire.

Danish Häagen–Dazs ice cream is one of the greatest success stories of the last few years – sales worldwide are over $100 million. However, its inventor wasn't Danish or even Scandinavian. He was a Polish immigrant to the US called Reuben Mattus. He chose the association with Denmark because he believed this was a country which no one in the world actually disliked. The name is completely fictitious and doesn't mean a thing (there's not even an umlaut in Danish).

In 1850 seventeen-year-old Levi Strauss set out from New York to San Francisco to seek his fortune, selling tents to miners during the California gold rush.

With no interest in his tents, Strauss decided to turn them into trousers, hardy enough to last given the miners' rugged lifestyle. These canvas trousers were popular and miners used to call them by the name of their creator – Levi's.

A few years later the same trousers were made from denim, which was still durable but softer. Levi dyed them blue so they wouldn't show stains and soil so much and they became even more popular. Their only complaint was that the pockets used to rip at the seams. This was remedied in 1873 by the addition of copper rivets at all the stress points – a hallmark of the company's products (the original versions had 501 rivets – hence the name Levi's 501s).

McDonald's isn't a made-up brand name. It was actually founded by the two McDonald brothers, Mac and Dick. Their first restaurant was a drive-in burger bar established in 1940 in San Bernardino, California. By 1948, frustrated at how much they were paying chefs, waiters and dishwashers, they radically changed the way they did business.

Out went an extensive menu and in came a limited number of options, fast service, low prices and no tipping. By 1952 the new-look McDonald's was a phenomenal success; their operating costs had been halved and they decided to franchise the system.

Meanwhile, a milkshake machine salesman called Ray Kroc had become well acquainted with Dick and Mac and the way they did business. In 1952 he became their first franchisee, opening a McDonald's in Des Plaines, Illinois. By 1961 he'd bought them out completely for $2.7 million. This meant he owned the trademarks, copyrights and all their trade secrets.

The McDonald brothers kept their original restaurant but had to rename it Mac's Place. A few years later Ray Kroc opened a McDonald's opposite them – and forced them out of business. He has been quoted as saying: 'It's ridiculous to call this an industry. This is rat eat rat. Dog eat dog. I'll kill 'em before they kill me. You're talking about the American way of survival of the fittest.'

Kroc died in 1984, one of the richest men in America. Today the company has outlets in over 100 countries, and is the largest owner of retail property in the world.

. Coca-Cola was originally developed as a medicine by a confederate officer turned chemist called John Styth Pemberton. He adapted it from an earlier concoction called French Wine Coca, which he advertised as 'the ideal brain tonic', when prohibition was declared in the southern states. The name Coca-Cola was invented later, based on the fact that it then contained the dried leaf of the coca plant – a principal source of cocaine.

It was originally marketed as 'The Intellectual Beverage and Temperance Drink' and was flat rather than fizzy. Pemberton also hinted rather broadly that it might also be a very potent aphrodisiac. It was Pemberton's accountant, Frank M. Robertson, who invented the name and world-famous logo. Still nothing very much happened with Coca-Cola and, in 1887, Pemberton sold two thirds of his company shares for just $283.29. Later, the formula was sold to Willis Venable, who had the idea of adding soda water to the concoction. He sold it for $2,000 to Asa G. Candler, who then sold it to a group of Atlanta businessmen in 1919 for the slightly larger sum of $25 million.

Today, the precise formulation for Coca-Cola, referred to as 'Merchandise 7X', is still one of the most closely guarded secrets in the world, and no more than three people know the fifteen secret ingredients at any one time. These three never travel together in case they're kidnapped or involved in a fatal accident. The drink has never been patented, because this would mean revealing the exact contents, and the formula itself is kept in a top-security vault somewhere in Georgia. Today, it is sold in more countries than there are in the United Nations.

Pepsi-Cola, on the other hand, was invented by a pharmacist called Caleb B. Bradham. He originally called it 'Brad's Drink'. It became Pepsi-Cola in 1893 when he decided it was good for combating dyspepsia. Incidentally, Cambodians now use the word 'Pepsi' to describe a loud and spectacular explosion. During the civil war in Cambodia, Pepsi's lorries were commandeered by the government and the brightly coloured vehicles became a popular target for Khmer Rouge rocket attacks. Apparently, a truck full of soda bottles blowing up is a real sight to see ...

In recent years, a Pepsi-Cola advertising campaign in China was hurriedly pulled after it was discovered that the company slogan 'Come Alive With Pepsi' translated to 'Pepsi brings your ancestors back from the grave'. Coca-Cola faired slightly better. When their famous slogan 'It's the Real Thing' was translated into Chinese, it baffled the entire population. Somehow it got translated as 'The Elephant Bites the Wax Duck' ...

The shopping trolley was invented by Sylvan Goldman, a grocery store owner from Oklahoma. He noticed that customers stopped buying items as soon as their hand basket got too heavy, and introduced the shopping trolley which he called the 'Basket Carrier'. At first his customers were not too sure about the newfangled invention but, undaunted, Goldman employed six people to pretend to be customers and to do nothing all day but push their shopping trolleys about and put items into them. Encouraged by other shoppers seemingly using the trolleys, the public soon followed suit.

The invention netted him $400 million and was so popular that, at one point, there was a seven-year waiting list for supermarkets wanting them ...

£. Parker Brothers initially rejected Monopoly, the world's best selling board game. They told inventor Charles Darrow, an unemployed heating engineer from Philadelphia, that it contained no less than fifty-two fundamental playing errors. Luckily for them they changed their minds. The game made Darrow a millionaire and he was able to retire at the age of forty-seven and devote all his time to growing rare orchids.

£ Erno Rubik achieved multimillionaire status by driving people nuts. There were 43,252,003,274,489,856,000 different ways of aligning the coloured squares in his puzzle cube and over 100 million were sold worldwide at between £4 and £6 each soon after its release.

Although Rubik designed the Cube in 1974 as a puzzle for his students (he was a Hungarian architectural professor), it wasn't marketed until 1980 in America. While most people gave up after a short while, fanatics worked out how to solve the puzzle in less than a minute, some in under thirty seconds.

One woman even filed for divorce citing her husband's infatuation with the Cube.

£. Sales of the Teenage Mutant Ninja Turtles products grossed $400 million wholesale in 1990. At the time, 90% of American boys between three and eight owned at least one Turtle toy. The multimillionaire creators of this fad were Peter Laird and Kevin Eastman, two struggling freelance comic artists who shared a house together. At the time when they invented the characters in November 1983, twenty-nine-year-old Laird earned money for his rent by illustrating vegetables for the garden section of an East Coast newspaper while Eastman was working as a short-order cook.

They drew the characters just for fun, combining two 'hot' trends in comics at the time – mutants and ninjas – gave them art-history names and invested $1,500 in printing 3,000 copies of a one-off comic which they launched via a home-made press release in May 1984, stating that this was 'the first real comic book to be published in New Hampshire – at the Howard Johnson's Motor Lodge'. This sold out, so issue two followed. Then issue three. Need I go on?

At the peak of Turtlemania, over half a million copies of the comic were being sold each month and the movies and merchandise grossed hundreds of millions of dollars worldwide.

Divorcee Bette Nesmith Graham went to work in 1951 to support her son. She found work as a typist but, unfortunately, she wasn't a very good one. She tried to erase any mistakes with a pencil rubber, but this just smudged the carbon from the typewriter ribbon. She then hit on the idea to cover them up, concocting her own water-based white paint which she applied with a small brush.

Soon, a lot of the secretaries at her office wanted to use the mixture and she spent all her spare time refining it at home, using her kitchen as a laboratory and her garage as a factory. All the time she kept working, educating herself in business matters including marketing and promotion. Eventually she left her job and began to sell small bottles of the white correcting fluid called 'Mistake Out'. She offered it to IBM but they turned it down.

By the late 1950s demand had skyrocketed. She upped the production at home, changed the name to 'Liquid Paper' and applied for a patent and a trademark. In the late 1960s she started a factory and by 1975 she employed 200 people and sold twenty-five million bottles of Liquid Paper in thirty-one countries. Four years later the Gillette Corporation bought Liquid Paper for $47.5 million plus royalties. Over here we know the product as Tipp-Ex.

If you think there's something familiar about Bette Nesmith Graham's name, you're right. Her son is Michael Nesmith, the bobble hat-wearing member of The Monkees. As a child he spent all his spare time scrounging up old bottles which his mother could use to sell the formula in.

The invention of the sandwich came about because of the Earl of Sandwich's bad habits. He was a compulsive gambler and, once at the table, could not be tempted away. During one marathon twenty-four-hour gambling session, he asked a waiter to bring him two pieces of bread and a slice of ham. When the waiter returned, the Earl slipped the ham between the two pieces of bread and crammed the whole thing into his mouth to save time.

John Logie Baird made the first TV receiver from an old electric motor, a tea chest, biscuit tin, cardboard, piano wire, string, sealing wax, glue, a cycle lamp lens and some needles.

Fed up with his ten-year-old son John leaving deep furrows in his lawn whenever he rode his tricycle, a Scottish vet invented a new kind of tyre to stop the damage to his grass. The new invention became known as the pneumatic tyre – and the little boy's father was called John Boyd Dunlop!

When Prince Arthur of Connaught was at Eton he wrote to his grandmother, Queen Victoria, asking if she could send him £5 so he could buy extra tuck at the school shop for Christmas. The Queen refused, telling him to curb his expensive tastes. The prince then replied telling her not to worry. He had sold her letter to another boy for £7.

Chapter 11

THERE HAS TO BE A BETTER WAY!

> *What's the use of money if you have to earn it?*
> *— George Bernard Shaw*

From the previous chapter it would appear that all it takes to make your first million is one original idea. But, if you ask me, some of the following ideas are just a little too original ...

For example, the nephew of the celebrated French philosopher, Albert Camus, has put his thinking cap on

– and come up with a unique new form of power which he believes we may all be using one day. Nelson Camus astonished scientists in 1992 when he unveiled a battery powered by human urine. One Neltron-Nithium-Urine-based Cold Fusion Reactor Battery (which looks just like a rain barrel full of urine to the uninitiated) – filled with five gallons of urine, can, it was claimed, meet all the energy needs of an average family home for up to five days! Better still, if the donor of the urine eats generous helpings of garlic and onions, the electric potential of their wee increases threefold.

Camus has also created urine-powered batteries for cars. If the urine-powered home power plant ever gets commercial backing it could be an exciting breakthrough – but don't hold your breath. On second thoughts, perhaps you should ...

. One money-making idea that's surely a cut above the rest is the one pioneered by American medical company Organogenesis Inc. They make human skin replacement patches – out of severed foreskins left over after circumcision. Somehow, they can produce in the region of 200,000 three-inch discs of replacement skin out of a single prepuce ...

A strange German entrepreneur named Helen Wolfe is trying to get rich by selling mints containing drops of human blood. The mints come in four flavours – O, B, A and assorted. Helen says that Type A is the nicest because 'they taste like salty watermelon'.

. William Calderwood of Peoria, Arizona, has patented helium-filled furniture that can be floated to the ceiling when not in use to give extra floor space.

£ **Force-sensitive, music-playing condoms would be rather a distraction, don't you think? Inventor Paul Lyons of Southbridge, Massachusetts, however, thinks otherwise and has been developing a range since 1992.**

. In some parts of China, entrepreneurs have established a dating agency with a difference: they introduce dead people to one another. It's considered unlucky to have died unwed so, to guarantee a better (and less lonely) afterlife for any recently departed spinster or bachelor, relatives employ the services of 'dead dating agencies'.

£ Bryan Patrie of Menlo Park near San Francisco is the brains behind The Intelligent Toilet Seat. It uses infrared beams and warning lights to remind men to put the seat down after use. According to Bryan, this device could 'save marriages'.

. Elvis Presley was not Colonel Tom Parker's first shot at the big time. Before he met the King, the Colonel had an act called 'Colonel Parker's Dancing Chickens'. The act involved – well – chickens that danced (albeit because they were standing on an electrically heated hotplate). It was Elvis who brought in the real money, and saved a lot of chickens from very unhappy lives.

In Victorian times, an entrepreneur named Wulff patented one of the strangest devices of all times. He named it 'Wulff's Improved Apparatus for Throwing Animals in the Air for Exhibition Purposes'.
The name says it all.

. Juan Cordova and accomplice José Guzman were arrested in Lima for fraud, just before they could unleash their money-making-scheme on the rest of the world. They'd been collecting used condoms from parks, beaches – anywhere they could find them really – washing them out and re-packaging them as new.

£ A Korean grocer called Chung Kyu-Chil told police from his hospital bed that he had passed out unconscious after a heavy night drinking – and awoken to find someone had stolen both his feet. Knowing that the black-market value of second-hand grocer's feet was not particularly high, the police were quite suspicious. They subsequently discovered that the grocer had taken out twenty-four insurance policies that would net him over $1.7 million if he became disabled.

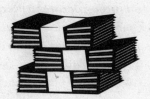

Chapter 12

SHORT ARMS AND LONG POCKETS

*It's rude and inconsiderate to overtip. It only
makes life more difficult and embarrassing
for people who are not as rich as I am.*
– J. Paul Getty

It seems to be a recurring pattern that the more
money people make the less they actually want to
spend. People who were probably reasonably generous before they had money become incredibly stingy
once their bank account gets into the black. And, if
they make really serious money, trying to get anything
at all out of them is like drawing teeth.

When John Paul Getty III was kidnapped in Italy in 1973, his billionaire grandfather initially refused to pay the $2.8 million ransom, claiming: 'I have fourteen other grandchildren and if I pay one penny now, then I will have fourteen kidnapped grandchildren.'

During the time he was kidnapped his grandfather spent $6 million on art at Christies and the ransom was only paid when John Paul Getty III's ear was cut off and sent with another ransom demand.

Incidentally, at the time, the Italian postal workers were on strike and the mouldy ear had sat in the post-box for two weeks!

. American shipping tycoon Daniel Ludwig was incensed when an employee had the audacity to send him a report that had been fastened with a paper clip.

He severely reprimanded the man, claiming: 'We don't pay to send ironmongery by mail!'

To save money on tipping cloakroom attendants, Aristotle Onassis refused to wear a coat. Because of his wealth he was expected to tip $5 each time he checked his coat. In addition, he would be expected to buy a very expensive coat and have it insured. All in all he reckoned that by not having a coat, he saved $20,000 a year.

. Despite being incredibly rich, French novelist Victor Hugo was also incredibly stingy, and made his wife and daughters live on a tiny allowance. Hugo, who liked to write standing up and in the nude, is also credited with sending the shortest – and therefore cheapest – telegram of all time. Wanting to find out how his new novel *Les Miserables* was doing, he sent his publishers a telegram simply saying '?' They responded with an equally short telegram. It said '!'

When Jean Paul Getty discovered that it cost him sixpence every time someone flushed a toilet on board one of his oil tankers, he had all the plumbing changed so that the toilets used sea water instead of fresh …

Guests who complained of the cold at Getty's home, where he kept the heating way down low or even off most of the time, were advised to keep their coats on.

Another example of his 'careful' attitude with money came when he calculated the wages of his gatekeeper. He did this by counting the number of times his main gate was opened and closed on a given day, then multiplied this number by 'a minute sum' (his words) to arrive at what he felt was an appropriate salary.

The industrialist John D. Rockefeller was legendary for his meanness. The *Charleston Gazette* once said of him: 'We saw a picture in the paper the other day of a little girl to whom John D. Rockefeller gave two dimes. It may have been only a co-incidence, but on the same day the price of gasoline went up one cent …'

George Bush avoided paying income tax in the District of Columbia while he was President of the United States on the grounds that he was living in Texas. In this case he successfully claimed that his home was a Houston hotel room – in which he spent only a few nights each year.

Despite all his wealth, Clark Gable was a cheapskate when it came to his false teeth. He bought a really cheap and ill-fitting pair that clicked incessantly as he talked. He didn't care – but it drove his then girlfriend Grace Kelly to distraction, and she decided to marry Prince Rainier of Monaco instead.

. To discourage visitors from helping themselves to his cigars, millionaire inventor Thomas Edison once had several boxes of custom-made panatellas filled with cabbage leaves. One puff of these foul cigars was enough for even the most dedicated smokers – to Edison's delight.

The joke rebounded on him when his wife accidentally packed a box of these disgusting panatellas for her husband to take on a long business trip to the West Coast. Stuck on the train for days on end, and utterly desperate for a smoke, Edison had no choice but to smoke the cabbage leaf cigars himself.

John Christie, the wealthy founder of the Glyndebourne Festival Opera, was a great believer in buying in bulk to save money – even if his purchases were a little 'eccentric', like the 2,000 pairs of white plastic dancing shoes which he bought because he felt they 'might come in handy'.

He would come home from shopping with three umbrellas, or several pairs of silk pyjamas – just because he got a discount on them. His wardrobe contained 130 pairs of socks, over 200 shirts and 180 handkerchiefs. Once one of his staff asked him for a new typewriter but he was told instead to buy six on the basis that, 'I'm sure we shall need them.'

Christie's greatest extravagance was buying a ton of sugar in America just after the Second World War and bringing it back to England on the Queen Mary. At the time rationing was still in force and it was illegal to bring such a large quantity into the country. To get round this Christie persuaded his fellow passengers to bring small amounts of sugar through customs in their hand luggage. He then retrieved it all, loaded it into a waiting lorry and took it back to Glyndebourne where it was secretly stored in a cellar.

However, despite his great wealth he was also very cost-conscious. He always steamed off stamps that the Post Office had failed to postmark. He refused to tip waiters and porters. He travelled third class on the train and he worried so much about wasting electricity that he employed a servant just to turn the lights off after him.

£ **Sir Lew Grade was constantly horrified by some of the costs incurred by his productions. While making *Jesus of Nazareth* with Robert Powell he was mortified to learn there were twelve apostles. 'Twelve!' he shouted. 'So who needs twelve? Couldn't we make do with six?'**

After losing money on his expensive flop *Raise the Titanic*, he commented woefully, 'It would have been cheaper to lower the Atlantic ...'

£. The Kennedy family matriarch Rose never tipped service staff like waiters, taxi drivers, bell boys or maids. Instead she would hand them a small card which had a photograph of President Kennedy on the front and one of his favourite lines from the Bible on the reverse. She autographed these cards and handed them out instead of tips.

Other examples of her tightfistedness were her habits of buying cosmetics, using them and then returning them to the shop 'as new' for a refund, and she always remembered each of her twenty-nine grandchildren's birthdays – and gave them all a $15 cheque.

£ Some people just don't know how well off they are.

French landowner Samuel Tapon had a personal fortune of £1.5 million and a reputation for driving a hard bargain. After he lost the relatively small sum of £50,000 in a bad speculative deal he got severely depressed; in fact he felt so wretched that he decided to commit suicide.

Without giving away his feelings he walked into his local hardware shop and bought the rope that would end it all. A good businessman to the end, he managed to knock a few centimes off the price. Pleased with his bargain, he took the rope home and hanged himself.

. In the 1820s the title of London's most famous miser went to John Neild. He inherited a fortune from his property-owning father – but not his generosity. Neild's father was known as a philanthropist, a pubic-spirited gentleman who campaigned for prison reform. The only cause his son John supported was avoiding spending any money while building up his wealth.

Despite having a large house in Chelsea's fashionable Cheyne Walk he only occupied one room and slept on bare floorboards. He reduced his staff to one old housekeeper who had to get by on a pittance. Neild wore the same set of clothes day in, day out – a blue swallow-tailed coat with brass buttons, brown trousers and patched-up shoes.

He refused to clean or even brush his clothes for fear of wearing them out and wouldn't spend money on the 'extravagance' of an overcoat, no matter how wet or cold the weather.

When it came to collecting rent from his tenants he refused to pay commission to an agent, insisting instead on visiting them himself. He caught lifts on farm carts and stayed overnight at his tenants' homes rather than pay for board and lodging. The rare times he was known to pay for a carriage, he chose the cheapest seats, on top and in the open. And when it stopped at a village to change horses he stayed freezing in his seat rather than spend money at an inn.

Due to a lifetime of meanness he doubled the fortune his father left him – an estimated £20 million in today's terms. After he died in 1852, Neild left it all to one person – Queen Victoria, 'for her sole use and benefit, and not her heirs'. It was rumoured at the time that she used this to buy Balmoral Castle in Scotland.

Do you know the reason that Groucho Marx adopted his trademark beret? It wasn't anything to do with fashion or style – it was so he could avoid checking in his hat, and tipping the hat check-girl at restaurants.

£ **In February 1953, the legendary tight-fisted American comedian Jack Benny went into a London bank to cash a cheque for $50. He had no proof of identity on him, so the bank manager said, 'I suppose the only way you can prove you're Jack Benny is by telling me a few jokes'. Jack immediately put the cheque away in his pocket. 'If I were to tell you jokes for fifty dollars,' he said, 'you could be sure I wasn't Jack Benny!'**

The American engine driver Casey Jones was killed on 30 April 1900. Rather than jumping to save his own life, he stayed at his post, slowing his locomotive down to save his passengers. His courage inspired a couple of already very wealthy composers to write a song in his honour. The song went on to earn them a quarter of a million dollars. To share their good fortune with Casey Jones' widow, they sent her a gift – a biscuit barrel. She later told a reporter from the *Philadelphia Examiner*, 'I'm grateful and wish them no more harm than that, in the next world, they should be coals in the furnace of my late husband's locomotive ...'

£ Cary Grant had a reputation for being one of the meanest men in Hollywood and was so tight that his friends gave him the nickname 'El Squeako'. To stop his servants taking advantage of him he is said to have counted the number of logs in his mansion's wood store and used a pen to record the level of milk in the milk bottles in his fridge.

Chapter 13

THERE'S HOPE FOR US ALL

> *A young fellow asked an old rich man how he
> made his money. The old guy fingered
> his worsted wool vest and said, "Well, son, it was
> 1932. The depth of the Great
> Depression. I was down to my last five cents. I
> invested that five cents in an apple. I spent the
> entire day polishing the apple and, at the end of the
> day, I sold the apple for ten cents. The next morning,
> I invested those ten cents in two apples. I spent the
> entire day polishing them and sold them that
> evening for twenty cents. I continued this system for
> a month, by the end of which I'd accumulated a
> fortune of $1.37.
> Then my wife's father died and left us
> two million dollars."*
> —Traditional joke

In amongst all the hard-luck stories of people who just missed out on millions, or of people who really didn't deserve to receive any millions in the first place, are the stories of people who were just incredibly lucky. Somebody up there seemed to be smiling down at them for just a few brief seconds and completely changed their lives beyond all recognition.

For example, Judy Garland became a multimillionaire and film star entirely by accident. MGM boss Louis B. Mayer had seen a very plump Judy Garland, then just fourteen, singing in a short film called *Every Sunday* with fifteen-year-old Deanna Durbin.

Leaving the screening, Louis B. Mayer told his aide to 'sign up the flat one'. He was referring to Deanna Durbin, whose singing was flat. However, his aide thought he'd said, 'Sign up the fat one' – and that's how Judy Garland got her big break!

In 1937, shortly before her death, Daisy Singer Alexander, heir to the Singer sewing machine family, made out her will, sealed it in a bottle and threw it into the River Thames. It read: '*To avoid any confusion, I leave the entire estate to the lucky person who finds this bottle, and to my attorney Barry Cohen. Share and share alike.*'

Twelve years later an unemployed man, Jack Wrum, was wandering along a San Francisco beach when he found the bottle. He took the contents seriously enough to take it to a lawyer who, after checking, confirmed that Jack was indeed Daisy's beneficiary. He inherited $6 million right away and $80,000 income every year from shares in the company.

Joseph Crowley won £2 million on the Ohio State Lottery. He promptly quit his job as a construction worker and set off for

Boca Raton in Florida to enjoy the good life — and to scoop £13 million on that state's lottery too!

Next time you go to a car boot sale bear in mind what happened to an anonymous middle-aged financial analyst from Philadelphia in 1989.

He paid $4 for a painting at a flea market but didn't even like the picture; it was the frame that caught his eye. When he took the back off, a folded piece of paper fell out. It was a copy of the Declaration of Independence, which he kept, mainly out of curiosity.

A few years later he showed it to a colleague who felt that although it was a copy, it still might be valuable. It was. It turned out to be one of twenty-four surviving copies made of the Declaration only a few hours after it had been drafted. This was by far the best, having been sealed in mint condition at the back of the picture frame for nearly 200 years.

The man sold it at auction in 1991 for $2.4 million.

The Swedish newspaper *Expressen* gave $1,250 to each of five financial analysts and a chimpanzee to see who could make the most money on the stock market in a month. At the end of the contest Ola, the chimp, was declared the winner, with a profit of $190. She had chosen her investments by pointing at random to company names on a list.

Like most rock millionaires, the journey to megastardom for Guns 'n' Roses was a long one. Before they hit the big time the group members all shared a dingy Los Angeles apartment and heated hamburgers over a fire made from burning drumsticks.

In July 1977, Melchor and Victoria Javier of Mamila ordered a $1,000 bank draft from the Mellon Bank of Pittsburgh, Pennsylvania. The folks at the bank got their zeros a bit muddled up and ended up sending the Javiers a cheque for $1 million. Immediately, the Javiers spent $750,000 of it on anything they could think of – and then challenged the bank to get it back!

As of March 1999, Britain's National Lottery had created 755 new millionaires. According to statistics, their car of choice is the Mercedes and they celebrate their winnings with holidays in Florida. Strangely enough, someone in Croydon has a ticket worth £2 million which has never been claimed. By the time he or she reads this, however, it will be too late …

Albert Einstein failed the entrance exam to Zurich Polytechnic when he was sixteen.

Fred Astaire's legs were insured for a million dollars. An MGM talent scout once assessed Astaire, saying: 'Can't act. Can't sing. Slightly bald. Can dance a little.'

Despite being universally recognised for his wit and learning, Noel Coward admitted that he'd had a poor formal education. During a TV interview to celebrate his seventieth birthday,

Coward said: 'I learnt all I know at Twickenham Public Lavatory.' Quickly, he corrected himself, saying, 'I mean Twickenham Public Library.' Then added, 'Oh dear! Quite a Freudian slip there, I'm afraid ...'

 Even the staff of millionaires can earn fortunes.

The chauffeur for oil tycoon Mike Bendum built up his own fortune of $17 million by keeping a keen ear open for oil stock market tips while driving his boss.

Similarly, John Wendel, a porter to John Jacob Astor, had invested his savings in Manhattan real estate as advised by his employer, and left behind a fortune of $100 million.

An ex-US Cavalry officer and pencil-sharpener salesman, Edgar Rice Burroughs started writing at the relatively late age of thirty-six, after failing in virtually everything else he had ever turned his hand to. In the grip of a devastating mid-life crisis, he turned to outrageous fantasy to escape – and created Tarzan of the Apes ...

Irving Berlin never learned to read or write music. He hummed his compositions to a secretary, who then wrote them out 'properly'.

Charles Steen was a young geologist who went to a remote part of Utah in the 1950s to prospect for uranium. Life was hard and almost a year went by without a strike. By then his money had almost run out and his family were going without meals. Steen persevered though and eventually found a vein of uranium that was to make him a millionaire.

One of the first things he bought with his new-found wealth was a bank in Colorado which had once refused him a $200 loan.

💰. While learning his craft at the world-renowned Pasadena Playhouse, Dustin Hoffman was voted equal 'student least likely to succeed'. The other student who shared this dire prediction was Gene Hackman …

💷 **On 30 December 1985 Doris Barnett of Los Angeles took part in California's Big Spin lottery on live TV. She spun the wheel and watched in amazement as the ball settled in the £3 million slot. She was beside herself as the show's host Geoff Edwards congratulated her, but her joy turned to bitter disappointment after he noticed that the ball had actually fallen out of the $3 million slot and into the $10,000 slot.**

The host explained to an emotional Barnett that the rules stated that the ball must stay in the winning slot for five seconds. She was hustled out of the studio but subsequently sued the California lottery for the full amount of $3 million.

The case went to court, where jurors watched countless videos of previous contestants being declared winners in less than five seconds. They awarded her the $3 million she sued for, plus an additional $400,000 for 'emotional trauma'.

💰. In 1990 a couple bought a box of scrap recording tapes that Nashville's Columbia studio had sold an engineer between 1953 and 1971. They paid $50 for the lot and on playing them, recognised some of the singers. Columbia weren't interested in buying them back so the couple sold the box to Clark Enslin, owner of a small New Jersey record label, for the tidy sum of $6,000 in 1992.

He discovered that the tapes contained rare recordings of

Elvis Presley, Frank Sinatra, Louis Armstrong, Roy Orbison and
Jerry Lee Lewis. Estimated value of his $6,000 investment?
$100 million!

**£ Gary Cooper started his Hollywood career as a
cowboy stuntman, earning $5 a fall. By 1939, he was
earning half a million dollars a year.**

£. As he was clearing out his desk after being sacked, Frederick
Baum found an old football pools coupon. On impulse, the
Munich office worker filled it in – and subsequently won almost
a million deutschmarks!

£ The $500 that David Morrell paid to his lawyer was the best
$500 he'd ever invested.

In 1971 Morrell was a professor at the University of Iowa
who wrote *First Blood* in his spare time. Although an anti-war
novel, the book was extremely violent and became a bestseller.
The movie rights were optioned and dropped by countless
studios until eventually Warner Brothers made the hit film of
the same name starring newcomer Sylvester Stallone.

When Morrell sold the film rights he was earning $1,000 a month so the $500 charged by his lawyer to alter the contract was a considerable gamble. His lawyer wanted to include things like sequels and merchandising rights but Morrell didn't think this was needed. For a start, in the novel Rambo is killed so that would mean no sequels. Secondly, he couldn't see how a psychopathic killer would be merchandisable, or that he would even have any real appeal.

Fortunately for him, his lawyer persuaded him to make the change. A small amendment but one that made Morrell a millionaire.

The names Bennett Cohen and Jerry Greenfield might not mean much to you but their ice cream probably does. Ben and Jerry's has a multi-million dollar turnover making the two friends and founders extremely wealthy. Why did they start an ice-cream company? Well, they wanted to start a food business in the late 1970s and bagels was their first choice. They quickly abandoned this idea when they discovered that bagel-producing equipment cost $40,000 – way beyond their limited funds.

Rethinking their plans, they invested just $5 in an ice-cream making correspondence course, mixing the ice cream by hand in an old rented gas station in Burlington, Vermont.

It's amazing how being in the right place at the right time can set you on the road to stardom and mega bucks. Rock Hudson was a postman who one day delivered mail to Hollywood agent Henry Willson. Chatting to Hudson on one of his rounds, Willson was impressed with his looks and his manner and arranged for him to meet director Raoul Walsh – he directed Hudson's first film, *Fighter Squadron*.

Roscoe 'Fatty' Arbuckle, the silent movie star, was a plumber sent to unblock the drains of producer Mack Sennett, creator of the Keystone Kops. The two got talking and Sennett offered him a role in his next film.

Harrison Ford quit being an actor in 1970 to become a professional carpenter. He was around George Lucas's house, fixing some shelves, when the director suggested he try out for a part in *American Graffitti*.

Even Marilyn Monroe got her break by pure chance. She was working in an aircraft factory, spraying fuselages. She did this day in and day out until an army photographer happened to call in to take propaganda pictures to help the US war effort. Impressed by what he saw, the photographer recommended that Norma Jean (as she was then known) should contact a modelling agency in Los Angeles. The rest, as they say, is history.

Hugh Hefner created the first issue of *Playboy* magazine in 1953 on his kitchen table. To finance it he sold his furniture, borrowed money from friends and threw in $600 of his own. The issue sold 51,000 copies and from that humble beginning, the Playboy empire was founded.

Later in life, guests were welcomed to his sumptuous forty-eight room mansion in Chicago by a brass plate outside the front door with the inscription 'Si Non Oscillas, Noli Tintinnare'. That's Latin for 'If you Don't Swing, Don't Ring'.

The young Elvis Presley was fired after just one performance at the Grand Ole Oprey. Jim Denny, the manager, took him aside and said, 'Listen, son, you ain't goin' nowhere. You oughta go back to drivin' a truck.'

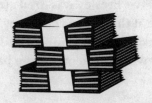 Claude Monet was only able to devote his life to painting because he won the French state lottery.

BEFORE THEY MADE IT ...

£ Sean Connery entered the amateur Mr Universe contest. He had previously worked as a bricklayer, a coffin polisher and a truck driver.

£ Alan Ladd was a hot dog salesman.

£ James Mason was a trained architect – as was James Stewart.

£ Cary Grant was an acrobat.

£ Goldie Hawn was a go-go dancer in a New Jersey strip club.

£ Charlton Heston was a nude artist's model, paid just $1.50 an hour.

£ Alfred Hitchcock was an electrical engineer.

£ Gene Hackman worked in a shoe shop.

£ Peter Stringfellow served in the merchant navy.

£ Charlie Chaplin was the caretaker of a music hall.

£ Jimi Hendrix was a paratrooper in the US Army.

£ Kirk Douglas was a parking lot attendant, a janitor and a hotel bell boy.

£ Roger Moore, now worth around £26 million, was a dish-washer.

£ Perry Como used to be a barber.

£ Bob Hope was a boxer.

£ Elvis Presley used to be a truck driver.

£ Dean Martin worked in a steel mill.

£ Boxer George Foreman worked on an electronics assembly line.

£ Clark Gable was a lumberjack.

£ Aristotle Onassis once worked as a telephone operator.

£ Gary Cooper used to be a baby photographer.

£ Dustin Hoffman was a teacher.

£ Sting used to be a primary school teacher. He's now worth £85 million.

£ Lou Costello used to work in a hat shop.

£ Richard Burton was a haberdasher's apprentice.

£ Al Capone was a used furniture salesman.

£ Ronnie and Reggie Kray were Alvin Stardust's agents.

£ George Michael used to work at British Home Stores.

£ Mickey Rourke was a cinema usher.

£ Vic Reeves worked on a pig farm.

£ Boy George was a shelf stacker in Tesco. Tesco said his appearance was 'disturbing'.

£ Danny Kaye was an insurance agent.

£ Sylvester Stallone had a job cleaning out lion cages at the zoo.

£ Warren Beatty was a rat-catcher.

£ Rod Stewart was a grave-digger.

£ Mick Jagger was a porter in a psychiatric hospital.

£ Jon Bon Jovi made Christmas decorations.

£ Ozzy Osbourne worked in a slaughterhouse.

£ Rock Hudson sold vacuum cleaners before becoming a postman.

£ Burt Lancaster sold ladies lingerie.

£ Luther Vandross was a defective-merchandise clerk at a store.

£ Frank Zappa was an encyclopaedia salesman.

£ Chuck Berry was a hairdresser.

£ Mark Knopfler was a university lecturer.

£ Author Stephen King worked in McDonald's.

£ Groucho Marx wanted to be a doctor, but his parents couldn't afford to support him through college.

£ Cyndi Lauper cleaned out dog kennels.

Chapter 14

THEY ALMOST MADE IT...

> *If at first you don't succeed, try again.*
> *Then quit. There's no use being*
> *a damned fool about it.*
> —W. C. Fields

Alongside the thousands of men and women who have made fortunes from grasping the one nano-second opportunity in their lives, there is a sad list of others who had the moment but didn't recognise it for what it was.

Like, for example, Victor Fleming, the director of *Gone With the Wind*. Fleming turned down the offer of earning twenty per cent of the film's profits and demanded a flat fee instead.

'Do you think I'm a damned fool, David?' he furiously accused studio boss David Selznick. 'This picture is going to be one of the biggest white elephants of all time …'

Walter Hunt, a nineteenth-century American inventor, missed various boats, time and time again, in his lifetime. When it came to devising new products he had no shortage of ideas. His inventions included a machine to spin flax, a forest saw, a fire engine siren and a coal-burning stove. All these worked but he didn't make much money from them and was usually in debt.

He owed one particular friend $15 in 1849 and decided the best way to pay him back would be to invent something else. Hunt took a piece of brass wire about eight inches long, coiled it at the centre and shielded it at one end. Three hours later he'd just invented the safety pin. He took a patent out on this device and then sold the rights to it for $400. This meant he could pay his friend back and still have $385 left.

Then he watched his product go on to earn millions and millions of dollars for someone else …

The inventor of the zip sold his invention to a speculator for just £550!

John Ryan, creator of 'Captain Pugwash', got just £4 from the BBC for the pilot episode.

In 1968, a diver named Tom Gurr discovered the wreck of a fabulous Spanish treasure ship the *San José de Las Animas* off the coast of Florida. On board was $4 million worth of gold – and it all belonged to Tom, at least it did as far as he was concerned because it was found more than three miles off shore. The US Government didn't agree though. They said the limit was three miles from the outer reef, bringing the treasure ship firmly into Uncle Sam's mitts.

Tom spent five years fighting the government, without any success. The legal actions cost him a fortune – and he wasn't allowed to sell any of the treasure to pay for it. Finally, on New Year's Eve 1973, he snapped. He invited a TV news crew on board his boat, took them out to the site of the sunken wreck and tipped all £4 million worth of treasure over the side of the boat into the water again. 'If the government want it, let them get it!' he sneered.

Needless to say, the American authorities were not best amused. Tom was promptly arrested on Grand Larceny charges for illegally disposing of government property! To avoid going to jail, he was forced to mount a large and very costly salvage operation to retrieve the treasure a second time. The government duly took their fifty per cent, but between the costs of the salvage operation and all the court costs incurred, Tom saw almost nothing of his $2 million share …

. The modern-day match was invented by a chemist called John Walker in 1827. He deliberately didn't take out a patent on his design, and never benefited from his invention since he believed it was too important to the nation.

Similarly, Pierre and Marie Curie would not take out a patent on their method of producing radium, because they believed radium belonged to the world.

Towards the end of his life, the painter Paul Gauguin composed a letter that said, 'I am down and out, defeated by poverty.' In 1957, that letter alone sold for 600,000 francs and his paintings are today worth untold millions.

On a hot summer night in 1933, Jerry Siegel lay in bed, sweltering in the oppressive heat. If only I could fly up to where there was wind, he thought, and little by little, over the course of the night, the idea of a Superman came to him. The next day, he ran straight to his schoolfriend Joe Shuster's house twelve blocks away with the germ of the idea. Both were only seventeen years old.

Despite their confidence, almost every comic syndicate in America turned Superman down. The Bell syndicate thought it lacked anything special, while United Features rejected it as 'Rather an immature piece of work.' The hottest property in the world spent six years on the shelf before it was cut and pasted into a comic book format by Harry Donenfeld, who bought it for $130.

For that paltry sum, Siegel and Shuster sold all rights to Superman, and had no more claim on him – or any money their character generated. As their fortunes and health declined, they lived in relative poverty until DC Comics granted them a modest pension for creating a character which had earned them untold millions.

The German physicist, Wilhelm Roentgen, who discovered X-rays in 1895, died poor because he refused to make any money from this important medical discovery. Others have made fortunes from it since in all sorts of ways, including one group of less than scrupulous entrepreneurs who made an absolute fortune by selling 'X-ray proof underwear' to shy people around the world ...

211

Chapter 15

US AND THEM

> *Anybody seen on a bus after the age of thirty*
> *has been a failure in life.*
> *— Loelia, Duchess of Westminster*

Some people acquire huge sums of money and do a lot of good with it. Some people acquire equally large amounts of cash and do nothing but harm with it. Others simply have no comprehension of what life must be like for people who haven't got billions in the bank.

Some of the world's best-known millionaires have absolutely no idea of tact or sensitivity when faced with those in the world who have rather less than them. And some of the jobs they ask those around them to do are, frankly, unspeakable.

For example, a servant named Solomon Attefeld was awarded land that is now worth millions of pounds by King John for doing his job well. But the job doesn't sound much fun! He was officially titled 'The Royal Head Holder', and it was his duty to escort the Sovereign whenever he got on board a boat and to hold King John's head when he got seasick.

Spare a thought, too, for King Henry VIII's servant whose basic role in life was to be the official royal bottom wiper. His official court title was 'Groom of the Stool'!

How's this for a repetitive job? At Ferrières, the 10,000-acre estate owned by the Rothchilds near Paris, one servant was employed to do nothing but prepare salads. Mind you, it's probably marginally more interesting than the work undertaken by one of the maids employed by millionaire W. W. Crocker at his Hillsborough, California, estate. Her full-time job was just polishing the silver.

> 'The meek shall inherit the earth –
> but not the mineral rights.'
> – Jean Paul Getty

. A clumsy waiter spilt black coffee all over the actress Beatrice Lillie's new and very expensive evening gown. Quick as a flash she admonished him, 'Go. And never darken my Dior again!'

The first Marquis of Curzon's first trip on a London omnibus was also his last. He was livid, and later told his friends: 'I hailed one at the bottom of Whitehall and told the man to take me to Carlton House Terrace – but the fellow flatly refused!'

Baron Sackville-West learned that an acquaintance of his had recently acquired a dog, and found this most peculiar. 'But how is that possible?' he remarked. 'He doesn't own a park to walk it in!'

The Duke of Marlborough was in a similar state of confusion when his valet left his service. One of the valet's duties was to put toothpaste on the Duke's toothbrush for him. The day he left the Duke exclaimed to another of his servants, 'What's the matter with my damn toothbrush? It won't foam anymore!'

After his death in 1658, Mongolian emperor Shah Khan Jahan was buried standing up inside a pyramid-type tomb, with his hand sticking out of a hole in the side. Visitors to the tomb could then pay their respects by shaking the dead emperor's hand. The practice lasted for forty years – and then the hand dropped off …

. Just before the First World War broke out, the German ambassador to Washington, Count Bernsdorf, was invited to a dinner in his honour given by the millionaire socialite, Mrs Cornelius Vanderbilt. Given the start of the conflict, she had expected the Count to make his excuses for not being there and was poised to cancel the arrangements when, surprisingly, he announced he would attend. Mrs Vanderbilt had then to telephone all the other guests telling them that the dinner was still on – but on no account must they mention the war. Although they were not yet involved, Americans were beginning to take sides according to their ancestry and the dinner was potentially a recipe for embarrassment.

What Mrs Vanderbilt had not taken into account, however, were the feelings of her staff, who were either English or from the countries Germany had already invaded.

Fortunately, the dinner commenced normally. Soup was served and enjoyed, but no waiting staff seemed to be around to clear the dishes and serve the next course. On investigation Mrs Vanderbilt found a note in the kitchen signed by all her staff. It read: 'We the undersigned regret to inform you that we cannot serve the enemy of our respective countries. We have thrown the rest of your banquet in the dustbins along with everything else left to eat in the house. We hope you all enjoyed the soup since we all took great care to spit in it before it was served.'

The dinner party ended rather suddenly and the ambassador left for Germany rather sheepishly.

£ In 1603, a virulent outbreak of plague in London had Queen Elizabeth I scurrying for the relative safety of Windsor Castle. In a magnificent show of unity with her suffering people, she had a large gallows constructed on the battlements and warned that anyone who tried to get in the castle with her would be strung up …

. Lee Iacocca, the multi-millionaire former head of Chrysler, had a reputation for having deep pockets but short arms when it came to staff welfare. A popular saying within the company was: 'If you have lunch with someone who looks like Iacocca and sounds like Iacocca, rest assured – if he offers to pick up the check, then it's not Iacocca.'

He once cut bonuses for Chrysler employees while accepting $20 million in compensation when he lost his job. He explained, 'That's the American way. If little kids don't aspire to make money like I did, what the hell good is this country?'

> To find out how effective certain poisons were, Cleopatra tried them out on her slaves.

£. Edward VI, who reigned from 1547 to 1553, was a thoroughly naughty boy while at school. However, it was out of the question to cane the future king so, every time he got caught doing something wrong, another boy – named Barnaby Fitzpatrick – was caned in front of him. I expect that taught Edward a lesson …

£ A reporter once asked J. Paul Getty if it was really true that he was worth over a billion dollars. The tycoon thought for a short while before replying, 'Yes. I suppose it's true, but a billion dollars doesn't go as far as it used to.'

£. Peter III of Russia, husband of Catherine the Great, was a madman and a pyromaniac. Fearing what he might do while his wife was giving birth to their third child, her loyal manservant went and set fire to his own house. Peter ran off to watch the fire, whooping and hollering in delight, leaving Catherine to give birth safely.

£ **For twenty years, Walter Monckton loyally served Edward VIII, who later became the Duke of Windsor – without pay. To reward his twenty years of loyalty, Edward and Mrs Simpson gave him a cigarette case with his name engraved on it. To add insult to injury, they spelled his name wrong …**

£. At the time of Catherine the Great, a pedigree dog would set you back 2,000 roubles. A serf, on the other hand, could be picked up for 300 roubles …

Scott Fitzgerald: 'The Rich are different to us.'
Ernest Hemingway: 'Yes – they have more money.'

. In 1890, one per cent of the American population owned more possessions than the other ninety-nine per cent combined. Today, eight per cent of the American population own more than the total wealth of the remaining ninety-two per cent and the assets of the USA's 400 wealthiest people are equal to the total savings that every American combined has in all the commercial banks.

The eleventh Duke of Norfolk was nicknamed the 'Dirty Duke' and was equally famous for being one of the richest and one of the smelliest people in England. When his body odour became so bad that his servants couldn't cope anymore, they would get him fiercely drunk and then wash him while he lay in a drunken stupor on the floor ...

. Anton Greller's parents told him he would never amount to anything in his life. With his poor handwriting and sloppy grammar he'd be lucky to get a job digging ditches, they warned him. It obviously hurt the young boy deeply because when he grew up and became one of Belgium's most successful businessmen, he would send cheques for large sums back home to his parents – written illegibly and full of mistakes so that they couldn't cash them.

> **'Any man who has to ask about the annual upkeep of a yacht can't afford one.'**
> **– J. P. Morgan**

Monaco, the playground of the super rich, has been described as 'A sunny place for shady people.' The principality enjoys the record for the largest number of Rolls-Royces per capita in the world – one for every sixty-five of its inhabitants.

£ To take their minds off the 1897 economic slump, Mr and Mrs Bradley Martin held a ball at the New York Waldorf Astoria hotel that is estimated to have cost them up to $400,000. Only the most fabulously wealthy were invited. However the spectacle of the rich flaunting their decadent lifestyle so enraged the general public that the Martins had to flee to England, and never returned to the US.

£. Lord Crewe was as snobbish as he was rich and told his servants that they must always remain out of his sight after 10a.m. If he so much as caught a glimpse of a maid or a valet at his family home, Crewe Hall, they would be dismissed on the spot. They took this to heart – which is why none of his staff reported the fire that broke out late one morning, and which eventually burned the grand house to the ground.

£ The Queen was making polite conversation with a man at one of her garden parties. 'And what do you do?' she asked one attendee. 'I'm a photographer, Your Majesty,' the man replied. 'What a coincidence,' said the Queen, 'I have a brother-in-law who's a photographer' – referring to Lord Snowdon, who was then the husband of Princess Margaret.

'Even more of a coincidence,' said the man. 'I have a brother-in-law who's a queen.' By all accounts, Her Majesty didn't get it …

Chapter 16

YOU CAN'T TAKE IT WITH YOU

'*Where there's a will, there are relations.*
– Michael Gill'

All good things must come to an end, of course. Even millionaires die – eventually. Their wealth might mean that they can sometimes put off the end for longer than the rest of us but, sooner or later, the Grim Reaper gets them and their fortunes – often leaving absolute chaos behind.

Take, for example, Americans Sue and John Fallsoft who were delighted when they heard that a distant

and rather eccentric relative, Miss Amelia McCaby, had died leaving them $1 million. Their excitement was short lived, however. In order to collect the money, they first had to arrange to have Miss McCaby buried on the Moon …

By the time Mrs Martin van Butchell died, she and her husband hated each other. It's not surprising then that she willed her considerable private fortune to a distant relative and gave absolutely nothing to her husband. The money and goods and deeds were to be passed over 'the moment I am dead and buried'.

Mr van Butchell hatched a plan that was as ingenious as it was downright spiteful. He didn't have her buried. Instead, he had her embalmed, clothed in her finest dress and then put on public display every weekday in the drawing room of their home so that anyone could see she had not been buried …

Sandra West was a rich Beverly Hills socialite who died suddenly aged thirty-seven, leaving an estate of $3 million. She left most of this to her brother – on one condition: that she was buried in her lace nightgown and her Ferrari, with the seat reclining comfortably.

He carried out her wishes – and inherited her fortune. The car was covered in concrete so no one would be tempted to dig it up and steal it.

The tenth Duke of Hamilton, Alexander Douglas, wanted to spend eternity in style, so when an ancient Egyptian sarcophagus came up for sale, he bid for it furiously against the British Museum and purchased it. He then stored the sarcophagus away in his family vaults, leaving strict instructions that he was to be placed inside after his death. Time passed and, when the Duke finally did die in 1852, his executors attempted to follow his wishes – only to discover the Duke was too tall to fit in the sarcophagus. In the end, they had to saw off his feet to make him fit ...

> **You can't keep a good woman down. Eva Peron died in Argentina in 1952, then was exhumed and buried in Italy in 1955. In 1971, they dug her up again and reburied her in Madrid. She was finally laid to rest in the family crypt in Buenos Aires in 1976.**

A rich, unmarried New Yorker died in 1880 and left everything to his nieces and nephews – except seventy pairs of trousers. According to his will, each pair would be auctioned off to the highest bidder with the proceeds going to the poor of the city. The auction duly took place with each successful purchaser finding to their delight a $1,000 bill sewn into the back pocket.

It was probably out of guilt, but Mrs Myrtle Grundt, the widow of a wealthy Australian fur dealer, left a million Australian dollars to a pair of polar bears in her local zoo.

. A wealthy American banker gave his wife and son a final shock when his will was read out. 'To my wife and her lover,' it began, 'I leave the knowledge that I wasn't the fool she thought I was. To my son, I leave the pleasure of earning a living; for twenty-five years he thought the pleasure was mine ...'

George Bernard Shaw left almost $1 million when he died in 1950. A chunk of that he willed towards trying to establish a new British alphabet – one with forty letters.